MY STORM

THE CITY IN THE TWENTY-FIRST CENTURY

Eugenie L. Birch and Susan M. Wachter, Series Editors

A complete list of books in the series is available from the publisher

Edward J. Blakely My Storm

MANAGING
THE RECOVERY
OF NEW ORLEANS
IN THE WAKE
OF KATRINA

FOREWORD BY HENRY CISNEROS

UNIVERSITY OF PENNSYLVANIA PRESS

PHILADELPHIA

Published by
University of Pennsylvania Press
Philadelphia, Pennsylvania 19104-4112
www.upenn.edu/pennpress

Printed in the United States of America
on acid-free paper
1 2 3 4 5 6 7 8 9 10

Library of Congress Cataloging-in-Publication Data
Blakely, Edward James, 1938–
My storm : managing the recovery of New Orleans in the wake of Katrina /
Edward J. Blakely. — 1st ed.
p.   cm. — (The city in the twenty-first century)
Includes bibliographical references and index.
ISBN 978-0-8122-4385-7 (hardcover : alk. paper)
1. Blakely, Edward James, 1938– 2. Hurricane Katrina, 2005. 3. Disaster relief—
Louisiana—New Orleans. 4. Emergency management—Louisiana—New Orleans.
5. Urban policy—Louisiana—New Orleans. 6. City planning—Louisiana—New Orleans.
7. New Orleans (La.)—Politics and government—21st century.
I. Title. II. Series: The city in the twenty-first century.
HV636 2005 .N4 B53   2011
976.3'35064092—dc23   2011026052
[B]

Azor Randolph was my maternal great grandfather who lived as a slave leaving the Randolph Plantation in Georgia for freedom after the Civil War walking with his wife to California to find a new life. He lived well past 100 years, some say 107 others 113. He was my first hero. He was a horticulturalist, inventor and story teller. All of my family is grateful for the gifts of wisdom he bestowed on all of us. He taught us we can conquer anything we set our minds to and the future is only guaranteed to those that seek it—every day.

CONTENTS

THE SCALE OF THE HURRICANE WAS IMMENSE. THE POWER OF the direct hit on a city was stunning. The suffering of the residents was shocking. And the challenges of the recovery effort were unprecedented in American history.

Of necessity, therefore, the strategy to bring New Orleans back from the brink required the best urban minds and most skillful public sector managers the nation could identify. Fortunately the New Orleans city administration found a person whose background, experience, and dedication qualified him at that level—Ed Blakely.

I had known Professor Blakely by reputation as one of the nation's most creative urban planners and most respected academics. His writings on urban solutions have shaped many ideas and careers over the years. I observed from afar his work as an urban administrator and courageous activist in Oakland and other cities. But it was during the working sessions that followed the massive civil disturbances in Los Angeles in 1992 that I first had the opportunity to see Ed in action and to work with him. In part because of my work in Los Angeles, President Clinton asked me to serve as Secretary of the U.S. Department of Housing and Urban Development in his Cabinet. In that capacity I was able to collaborate with Ed once again, most importantly in designing policies to engage urban universities as "anchor institutions" in central city neighborhoods by applying their employment capabilities, academic assets, and community development potential.

When Ed was designated by Mayor Ray Nagin of New Orleans to coordinate the Katrina response, he asked me to chair the board of external advisors. From my experience at HUD, I knew that a city with daunting prospects in normal times would present heartbreaking challenges after an epic natural disaster. I also knew that Ed was one of the few leaders in the world who would be up to the task.

From the vantage point of the advisory committee—which met in New Orleans to review plans, to offer suggestions, and to make recommendations to state and national officials—I saw that Ed willed the city onto a path to recovery. He and his colleagues extracted the best ideas from competing plans, steered resources to priority needs, jump-started bureaucratic organizations, and most importantly generated hope and inspired confidence that the job could be done.

The experiences and insights which fill this book are important for policy makers, for academic urban specialists, and for public-minded citizens everywhere. Looking to the past, *My Storm* is a first-person historical record of one of the highest profile and most decisive American events of the last decade. In the present, Ed's account constitutes a study of the fragility and the value of these complex social systems we call our cities. Most importantly, anticipating the future, Ed makes us think about preparations in our own metropolitan areas for potentially massive disasters which may once have been unimaginable but which now appear with frequency in news reporting from around the world. Natural disasters and man-made destruction will be more damaging and tragic as they occur in increasingly populated areas of the globe. Ed counsels that we need to think ahead to prevent massive human suffering and that we must prepare far in advance for large-scale rescue and recovery efforts.

Ed has devoted his personal energies and career to making life better for people who live in the cities of our world. Most of the time that has meant Ed is planning for progress. It takes a wise man to know how to apply his ideals and personal courage to envision progress amidst a crushing setback. That wisdom must then be buttressed by the herculean determination to make sure that one step backward is always countered with two steps forward. Ed Blakely has always shown us how to take steps forward. In *My Storm* he shows us once again.

MY STORM

I ARRIVED IN NEW ORLEANS ON JANUARY 7, 2007, THE 192ND anniversary of the historic Battle of New Orleans. I had been called to take command in a new and perhaps more daunting battle, for the life and soul of the nation's most distinctive city. This was my first official day on the job as the "czar" to lead the post-Hurricane Katrina recovery effort.

New Orleans has one of the richest racial and cultural tapestries in the United States. It's where jazz emerged as an art form. It was a place of fame and fable. Tennessee Williams created splendid imagery for it. Marlon Brando gave it face and character in *A Streetcar Named Desire*. Great artists Louis Armstrong, Tina Turner, Josephine Baker, Mahalia Jackson, and Scott Joplin, and athletes such as football stars Marshall Faulk and the Manning brothers, were born or raised in the city.

For many personal and professional reasons, however, few of these greats called, or call, the city their current home. New Orleans is a gem woven into America's historic fabric. But New Orleanians, both black and white, prefer its fable, myths, and faded glory to grappling with the real issues and problems that afflict the city.

Long before Katrina, New Orleans had descended from the South's largest city in the 1940s and 1950s to a declining shell of a city by the 1970s, with rampant commercial and residential vacancies. It lost both luster and population to nearby Birmingham and Houston. The Mississippi River, the city's artery for commerce, has also been its demon. Overflowing its banks many times, the Mississippi nearly ruined the city in 1927, a fate averted only by blowing up the dikes near the city and conscripting some of the black community to fight the flood waters.

Mississippi floodwaters have brought the city trial by water. Hurricanes have been at least as daunting and damaging. Originating in the Gulf of Mexico, a huge hurricane tore New Orleans asunder on September 29, 1915. The local levee district stated in a report, "The . . . 10-foot levees that are protecting the city should be questioned as not being high enough after the passage of this storm." A parade of deadly hurricanes followed in the next half-century: Betsy in 1965, Bob in 1979, Danny in 1985, Florence in 1988, and Andrew in 1992, all preludes for Katrina in 2005.

Oil drilling and pumping in the Gulf of Mexico, which in the 1970s seemed to be the city's economic savior, removed ecologically valuable cypress swamplands, and the constant dredging and filling in of marshland has left the city even more vulnerable to storm surges that can overwhelm poorly constructed dikes. Although the U.S. Army Corps of Engineers technically supervised the New Orleans levees, five local levee boards oversaw this shoddy work.

By 1960, the New Orleans populace and political leaders had learned to play "victim" to their economic woes by settling into passivity. For example, the port failed to adopt the modern technology of container shipping; ongoing sagas of political corruption sent scores of local administrators and politicians to jail; and official mismanagement promoted the construction of homes and commercial structures on marshland. Oliver Houck of Tulane University is quoted in the *National Geographic*, "Locals wanted the cheapest possible protection system; but it wasn't cheap, it was just badly built." In the 1960s, when Miami was learning that sprawling into sensitive marshland could endanger the city, and steering construction from areas adjacent to the Everglades, New Orleans was expanding into environmentally dangerous swamps east of the city.

New Orleans has also played the victim to bad urban development by politicizing land use. Building permits were literally for sale in New Orleans. The city faced Katrina in late August 2005 with no up-to-date, comprehensive master land use and zoning plan, or even a decently staffed and funded professional planning department. When the storm hit, as Blanche said to Stella in *A Streetcar Named Desire*, "the searchlight which had been turned on the world was turned off again, and never for one moment since has there been any light that's stronger than this—kitchen—candle." It was to this candle of a city that I came in January 2007. New Orleans had almost no internal administration, no confidence, and little civic leadership.

Hurricane Katrina was a disaster of enormous size. Eighty percent of the city was damaged. No city in the United States had been that extensively destroyed since Sherman razed Atlanta during the Civil War. Most of New Orleans was underwater for 57 days. Millions of pounds of water were crushing the basic infrastructure of the city: pipes, electricity, and so on. Every institution was shuttered. Schools, churches—everything was closed. All property was damaged in one way or another in a land area equal to six Manhattans. Some had been smashed and then soaked by floodwaters that poured through poorly constructed levees and concrete ramparts knocked down by Katrina. Roughly a thousand people had died within the city limits, and half again as many in adjacent areas. Some 200,000 homes had been destroyed, many by cyclonic winds or raging water as flood defenses fell, others more slowly in the weeks before the putrid water could be pumped out of the bowl-like city. Almost without revenue of its own, New Orleans had been reduced to begging from Washington, D.C., to keep even rudimentary services intact. So the city was unsafe for habitation. Ten Superdomes of debris had been removed from the city by 2007, and more was to come.

But what made the Katrina tragedy truly epic couldn't be found in that recitation of facts and figures. It involved what I knew, but that many didn't or wouldn't say: the damage to New Orleans started long before the first levee broke. Some examples:

- The city was in poor physical shape, losing people every year since 1960, with deteriorating housing stock.
- The water system was pumping 200 percent of what customers needed, because the system suffered 50 percent leakage.
- There was no operating program for street repair in a city that was literally sinking. (All streets lie below sea level in a buckling flood plain.)
- There were few records of—or any way to determine—how much property the city owned, where it was, or how it was being used.
- The school system was just as broken, and had been taken over by the state in 2004.

My job as recovery czar was to "fix" the damage wrought by Hurricane Katrina. But I found these and other underlying problems to be far more compelling and challenging than the ravages of the storm itself.

My temperament was and remains to say it like it is. I try to do the job—not the one that's asked, but the one that's needed. I thus became a lightning rod for those who did not want to look at the real issues and preferred to present a past that was never as good as it sounded. As Nicole Gelinas of the Manhattan Institute for Policy Research, who knows the city well, observed in September 2005, "The truth is that even on a normal day, New Orleans is a sad city."

I found that many New Orleanians realized that their common problems predated Katrina. But I also found that in a city that is small and impervious to outside ideas, people don't challenge the establishment. "Speak out and be put out," as one television newscaster edified me shortly after I arrived.

Disasters tend to uncover nasty truths. New Orleans's true tragedy was its default position of denial, its fractious politics, and its resistance to discussion across the lines of disagreement and dissent.

In other words, much of the disaster had happened before the disaster.

This is the story of what I tried to do to help New Orleans save itself. It's a record not of everything that happened, but of the highlights and low lights.

The book is intended for general interest readers, business leaders and managers, politicians and would-be politicians, urban planning professionals and public policy administrators—and, by extension, managers in the public and private realms who deal with public issues. It is also a text for students entering management training, especially for those who aspire to public management and urban planning careers. The book is my deliberate follow-up to the great work of Jeffery L. Pressman and Aaron Wildavsky, *Implementation: How Great Expectations in Washington Are Dashed in Oakland; or, Why It's Amazing That Federal Programs Work at All . . . As Told by Two Sympathetic Observers Who Seek to Build Morals on a Foundation of Ruined Hopes.*

My title could mimic that one: *How Great Expectations in New Orleans Were Dashed in Washington*, with me as a sympathetic guide for the tale. But I'm not an observer. I'm the center of the story and the storyteller. My goal is to enrich the literature for all public- and private-sector managers and urban planners of every type, no matter where they practice in the world. The same pressures, conflicts, and character types that I depict in post-Katrina New Orleans exist everywhere that I've worked. The city's racial, economic, and social inequities are similar to those affecting most cities in the United States and many elsewhere in the world. Although Katrina was a horrific event, it was, from an administrative standpoint, similar to tragedies that I've observed or been involved with in many other places.

Much of the post-Katrina story is presented in Robert Olshansky and Laurie Johnson's *Clear as Mud*. My book picks up from where their story leaves off. They stop at the attempts to plan, and I depict the issues I encountered as we started to formulate and carry out the plans citizens and experts forged out of the cloudy mud and debris in the months before I arrived.

A theme running throughout this book is that although locals lamented the slowness of the recovery, their anger was misplaced. I surmised that the city was at death's door before Katrina hit. And even now, unless the real, preexisting problems of poverty, racial inequality, local bureaucratic incompetence, and a shallow economy are repaired, no dikes will save New Orleans, one of America's truly unique and formerly great cities.

In this narrative, I try to build on all these themes. It's my point of view and story, and my story alone. It comes largely from my weekly notes, which I've compiled on Sundays for more than sixty years. At times the notes were rough, so I sought additional information and perspective from friends and colleagues who shared the journey with me.

Chapters 1 through 5 provide some background on my career and how and why I came to New Orleans. In Chapters 6 through 9, I recount by theme the key elements of my work as recovery director once I arrived there. I consider both successes and failures, and try to assess our challenges and our work candidly. I look at the issues of planning, money, civic organizations, economy, media, race relations, funds, personnel, and geo-hazards of the city. The final three chapters reflect on and assess the New Orleans recovery, outline my recommendations for disaster recovery approaches in the federal government, and my own not so easy departure from the Big Easy.

The story of the post-Katrina recovery has lessons for all would-be and current policymakers. It is, perhaps, *a cautionary tale.*

PART I

Seeing the Problem

1. AN ALARMING VIEW FROM DOWN UNDER

I GOT MY FIRST VIEW OF HURRICANE KATRINA AND ITS devastation from computer news feeds in Australia. I had moved to Sydney with my wife Maaike, an Australian, in 2003. My goals were to retire—to Sydney, a city we both loved—and to fulfill a childhood aspiration to live outside the United States. Although we were comfortable financially, when the University of Sydney offered me a professorship and, with it, permanent residency, I accepted. I also started a consulting practice. With few cares in the world, we settled into a beautiful cottage in a nice town close to one of Sydney's most precious and beautiful beaches.

Early on the morning of August 30, 2005 (we're a day ahead of North America), my wife yelled at me from my home office to come look at what was going on in New Orleans: "You have to see this!" I went into the office and saw on television blurry figures and a bus. Some people got off the bus, and new people moved toward it. The difference was their color: blacks got off so whites could board. I couldn't make out what was going on.

"Where's the Army?" I mumbled.

"I don't know," she said, turning her head up and peering at me. "Where should they be?"

"They should be getting the people out," I said.

I went back to the bedroom and put on my running clothes. I wanted to get out of the house and clear my head of what I had seen on TV. I walked out onto the pavement by my large, shady oak tree. It was 6:50 a.m. My neighbor's door flew open, and he hurried to join me. "Morning, mate!" I said. "Are you ready to roll?"

"G'day Ed," he responded cheerfully.

"It isn't such a good day in New Orleans."

"Guess you're right," he volunteered. Like me, Frank is a professor at the university. But since we never see each other on campus we use our walks to talk about new developments there and in the world generally. We moved down the path in the park across the street toward the road that leads to the beach. It was late winter Down Under, and a characteristically beautiful Sydney day, a bit cool with fresh, clean air coming at us from the blue waters of Sydney Harbor.

Frank assumed I knew something about New Orleans. His first question was, "Is New Orleans all African American?"

"No. No major American city is," I replied. "However, the people you're seeing on TV are mostly poor, with many blacks too poor to get out of the city before the storm." He looked at me curiously, so I added, "In New Orleans, I mean."

When I got home from my walk, the radio was on. A couple of semi-hysterical Australian women were speaking on a phone hookup from a hotel in New Orleans. They told horrific stories of people murdered and raped at the Superdome, and they voiced fears that they'd be sent there. Could the situation be *that* bad?

My wife asked. "How can this be happening?"

I said nothing. I had no answer.

Then she asked, as she poured my morning cereal, "So, what are you going to do about it? Can't you call the White House or something?"

"Honey," I responded, with dripping sarcasm, "I am sure the President is aware of all this and help is on the way."

"No, you're wrong," she said. "Go look for yourself."

I did, and I saw the mayor of New Orleans on television. He was begging for help. "C. Ray Nagin," the caption read. There he stood, in a wet tee-shirt with a glistening bald head, asking the world for help.

My wife had followed me into the office. "This is different," she said solemnly. "Do something! You know people in Washington and many other places."

"Hmm," I replied. This was the first time I'd ever heard her refer to my various contacts as anything more than a nuisance.

Weeks went by, and the more I saw and read about what was happening in New Orleans, the more I felt that I *did* need to be involved, although I was now living many thousands of miles away. The city and its crisis wouldn't leave me alone—and, besides, I was part of a very select group worldwide: disasters are my specialty.

■ ■ ■

I had been in the planning and recovery business since the 1960s. I'd wanted to join the Peace Corps in 1963, following military service, but that wasn't possible because former military personnel couldn't serve in the Corps. Instead, I worked my way across the United States to get used to civilian life again. In lieu of the Peace Corps, I signed up to be a volunteer for the American Friends Service Committee (AFSC).

My assignment was in Italy, specifically the town of Villa Mimosa in Reggio Emillia. When I got there, I felt ready to get back to work. The villagers met me like the prodigal son, because they thought I was a trained engineer with building skills. A guy I'd met in the AFSC volunteer school had created that impression. His name was Jim Brown. Jim had arrived in the village several weeks before me, and had become a real man about town. He was dashing, tanned, handsome, and girls threw themselves at him. He was also savvy about the town rebuilding project.

I, on the other hand, knew nothing about Villa Mimosa or its needs. But when I awoke the first morning and went to the cattle trough where we washed up, I learned that my pal Jim had maneuvered me into the role of project architect-engineer-builder and leader.

"*You*, Kemo Sabe," Jim said with a big smirk, pausing for effect, "are going to rebuild the school and the town square. You are in charge, my good man."

Destiny had tapped me on the shoulder. From that point on, I was involved in planning. Using the GI Bill, I studied education, urban planning, and management at California's public universities, earning an MA at UC-Berkeley in 1963 and a doctorate at UCLA in 1970. I found my way to Oakland after stints as executive officer at Pacific Telephone, the U.S. Department of State as special assistant to the assistant secretary of state, the University of Pittsburgh (assistant to the chancellor), and UC-Davis (teacher-administrator and associate dean of agriculture). I got married and, at each of those places, did volunteer football coaching. In 1976, I returned to Berkeley as a professor. There, I was reunited with many former colleagues who worked in programs to promote economic development in low-income communities.

My first foray into the field of crisis management came in 1974 after I met Lionel Wilson, chairman of the Oakland Anti-Poverty Program. Lionel, a 5'5", athletic dynamo, was a former judge who'd gone on to become Oakland's part-time, poorly paid mayor. I'd known him for years. He was a mentor in my college days at UC-Riverside and later as a Berkeley grad student. We shared a love of sports, and our friendship matured on the Berkeley tennis courts.

When Lionel became mayor in 1978, he made me one of his advisors. He and Frank Ogawa, a longtime Asian American city councilman I knew, persuaded me to join the mayor's team pro bono. Both Berkeley alums, they asked me to act as their go-between to get university faculty and staff involved in policy issues facing the city. They didn't want to depend on the civil service city manager for all their advice. As I was about to leave our first three-way meeting, Frank said, "That isn't all we need. We have to change the members of many boards and commissions. So please find people to serve—and please serve on key commissions yourself."

I was dubious. "How can I do that?"

Frank grinned. "You will be the Mikado."

"Un-hunh. When vacancies or resignations occur you want me to be the fill-in person until we can identify an acceptable replacement. Right, I got it." Frank, a big bear of a man, grinned broadly. We all agreed, and I walked out with what resulted in a twelve-year commitment to serve when called on and to build a university-city partnership. The partnership became the largest and best funded of its kind in the nation.

When the Bay Area earthquake hit in October 1989, Wilson was in his last term as mayor. I joined him on the scene of the caved-in Cypress Freeway. As he struggled over the rubble, he said, "Get things organized, I'm busy here." I had no idea what he meant. But when I saw him again two days later, I had a plan in my hands for rebuilding the city center. As a result, my picture ran in the *New York Times*. "A Blessing in Disguise" was its story of how the earthquake would kick off a renaissance for Oakland's downtown.

Only two years later, with the earthquake debris barely cleared and new mayor Elihu Harris on the job, I accepted a similar role. Harris wanted to build on my university connections and put together a new public-private partnership for economic development, alongside our university partnership, that would improve the city's long-term economic outlook. At Harris's request, and this time as a *paid* advisor, I took on several important jobs, such as chairing the city's first employment and training commission. Many of these jobs were political, others economic, such as running the public-private operation known as Oakland Sharing the Vision.

And when the big fire in the Oakland Hills erupted in October 1991, Mayor Harris asked me to devise a plan to rebuild and to prevent a recurrence of this kind of urban conflagration. I took Jane Gross, the *New York Times* Bay Area correspondent, through the area. We discussed how this tragedy presented another opportunity to do things right.

On September 11, 2001, I was in Manhattan, headed downtown to an office building near City Hall, when terrorists piloted airliners into the World Trade Center. I had been in New York a bit more than a year. I was fairly well known by the leadership of the New York Regional Plan Association, so I became vice-chairman of the city's Civic Alliance to Rebuild Downtown.

■　■　■

Several weeks after Katrina, however, I hadn't gotten enlisted into the disaster. No one in the United States had contacted me, so I assumed that no one would. I was ambivalent about getting involved, in any case. As part of my consulting work, I was happy guiding the Sydney Regional Strategy Plan of 2004 to improve an already fetching city.

New Orleans's trials and tribulations still occupied the international news, however. Not surprisingly, my university colleagues peppered me with questions about what was going on and why the response to Katrina seemed halting and lame.

George Bush and Ray Nagin, odd bedfellows, were both prime targets of the criticism I heard. The U.S. government is bewildering to outsiders, and most of us can't explain it clearly. Remembering when the mayor of New York came on TV after September 11 and acted as though he was responsible for the world, "Sydneysiders" on the street and at the university wondered why Ray Nagin couldn't be like Rudolph Giuliani. In this fashion they criticized, and I fretted, for months.

Then, one morning in mid-September, I received an email from an American Planning Association (APA) official I knew from my work in Oakland and Los Angeles. He asked if he could give my contact information to people looking for help in the continuing Katrina crisis. I replied simply, "Sure."

By the end of the day, I was in the loop for a flurry of emails establishing that the APA would take some kind of action, but no one knew what or when. One of my colleagues in California, Ken Topping, had told the Planning Association that I was interested in getting involved.

Living half a world away, I was answering the whistle like some old quarterback trying to play another season. I was back in the disaster business.

IT WAS NATURAL FOR THE ASSOCIATION TO REACH OUT TO ME. When I moved to Australia, everyone acted as if I'd resigned from the world. But my Stateside credentials remained strong. In addition to being at or near the center of activity after the Oakland fire and earthquake, and after September 11 in New York, I'd written op-eds on disaster planning and an article on natural disasters, and had served on the APA board. So in early October 2005 I booked flights to Los Angeles, Chicago, and finally Shreveport, Louisiana, for a Katrina recovery workshop sponsored jointly by the APA and the Federal Emergency Management Agency, better known as FEMA.

I packed all my old slides and notebooks that contain my reflections on how I handled the Oakland and New York events. I planned to organize this material for my presentation on the plane and during my pre-workshop layovers in Los Angeles and Chicago.

In Chicago, I went by APA headquarters to chat with Association president Paul Farmer and get his impressions of New Orleans and his organization's role in the crisis. The APA has space on Michigan Avenue, in a structure that looks like a great and venerable fort with windows and parapets at the top to impart grandeur and style. It reminded me of the first big building I ever saw in downtown Los Angeles—back when Los Angeles still had a downtown. All the pre-World War II buildings were works of art, with brick facings and small statues arrayed along the façades.

Farmer is a respected and able leader of the APA. He's a tall, handsome man who exudes authority. He greeted me with a warm smile, recalling that, a few years earlier, I had given the keynote speech at the Association's national conference.

Farmer opened our meeting by saying, "Well, Ed, we offered to help the planning department and the mayor early on. We've been stymied." Looking downcast, he continued: "I'm a native Louisianan. I know the history of planning in New Orleans, and it's not pretty. New Orleans has never had a modern, comprehensive master plan. There were attempts to make the planning commission—not the city council—responsible for planning and zoning, but they failed." He leaned back in his chair. "So, post-Katrina is a major disaster, and the city needs a clear plan. We simply can't get any traction.

"There are good people down there—like Karen Fernandez and Steve Villavaso, who are well respected local consultants—but they have not been able to get the city to accept a forward-looking master plan. This is the time to push hard for one. We just asked to have a team of well-known volunteer planners go down there to assess what was needed to get a recovery plan in place."

My next stop was Shreveport, in the northwest corner of Louisiana. The city was cold and quiet. We passed a military air base that was also quiet—curiously so, because evacuees from the storm presumably would have been housed there. Curious, too, was the choice of the Sheraton Casino-Hotel as the location for the disaster workshop I was there to attend. A gambling casino, a metaphor for risk and chance, seemed either an apt location or an unfortunate pun for the prospects of New Orleans. Were many New Orleanians being housed or bivouacked in trailers or temporary shelters in the city? I took a walk to see for myself.

I saw very few pedestrians, and plenty of vacant hotels and apartment buildings. I was surprised. Why so little activity in a safe "catchment" area not too far from the storm? I remembered reading that New Orleans residents had been transported as far as Boston, while here, in their own state, a military base and vacant buildings could presumably have absorbed more than a few thousand. This would be a question for FEMA about where evacuees were sent and why.

I've led many workshops on community crises. It's my business. Here, however, except for talking about my Oakland experience, I was essentially a listener, a would-be learner. At the workshop, I spotted my friend James Schwab, from the APA head office in Chicago, and Ken Topping, former planning director of Los Angeles, well known for his post-disaster expertise. To my surprise, an insurance expert was present—Laurie Johnson, who usually works with large commercial firms after a disaster. The Louisiana APA delegation consisted of evacuees who were living with relatives or friends in a half-dozen states. But no one from the New Orleans planning department was present.

When I raised that point about no New Orleans planners to a young woman who'd worked at the department before the storm, she just shrugged her shoulders.

"Well," I said, "I bet they are doing the recovery plan."

"I bet they are not," she replied, and walked away.

The workshop crowd wasn't large—forty at most including the facilitators. Anxiety seemed to pervade the room. A simple presentation outlined the damages and issues. Laurie Johnson had the best information on the situation, and she recounted it. Other speakers gave other accounts as we moved through the day, and temporary, on-loan consultants from FEMA explained how the agency's planning process worked.

At lunch, I asked one of the FEMA reps, "Why are people being housed so far away from New Orleans?"

He studied me for a moment and replied, "I'm from Illinois, and I am just here on detail for this workshop. I haven't been to New Orleans." I almost fell out of my chair.

As the day wore on, small discussion groups formed. I joined one to hear some New Orleans Chamber of Commerce people discussing business losses in the city.

On the second day, I presented my Oakland story. I outlined the ways we had developed recovery plans for the earthquake and the fire in the hills. My basic points were that recovery must be based on a clear and coordinated strategy for future improvement, not just a plan to put things back where they were. As one of several illustrations, I cited the relocation of the badly damaged Cypress Freeway. I also discussed September 11 in New York as an example of strong early command and direction.

The workshops that followed focused on options for New Orleans's recovery. Sandra Gunner, a short, light-skinned African American, introduced herself as executive director of the New Orleans Chamber of Commerce. She and a Chamber colleague came over to chat with me. They asked if I might come to New Orleans at some future date. The colleague said, "I think you can be useful to us."

I also met Steve Villavaso, elected leader of the New Orleans APA chapter. Villavaso, a big man with a forceful speaking style, was already passionately engaged in the recovery planning process. He was advocating for a New Orleans master plan "with the force of law." I asked him what that meant, noting that "a master plan is a legal document with the full force of law."

He replied, "Not in New Orleans. The city council is the planning body there." That was news—and far from good news—to me.

I decided that I might be able to help Villavaso and Gunner work on an effective master plan for New Orleans in the wake of the storm. I could do that mostly at a distance, flying in three or four times a year at my own expense. Although the situation appeared grim, I knew that it was also an opportunity for New Orleans, and for me personally an opportunity to become involved once again in leading a city out of a very difficult and complicated situation.

The workshop proved useful. I'd met some significant players. At this point, however, I needed to catch a plane for an assignment in China. When I arrived there, I was asked by the senior officials who invited me how and why I was not helping out in New Orleans.

And by the time I returned from China to Australia, word was circulating in New Orleans that I was interested in coming there to survey the situation.

Not any time soon, I thought. The city was in too bad a shape to accommodate visitors. The political landscape wasn't much more hospitable. The national press was being mercilessly critical of the Bush administration and questioning every action taken in New Orleans. Why get caught up in a seemingly senseless fight with the federal government involving Louisiana? From my early days in Oakland and my work with the Clinton administration (on the San Francisco Presidio project and as an informal advisor to Housing and Urban Development Department, HUD), I knew that Louisiana was regarded poorly by Washington bureaucrats—and that New Orleans wasn't trusted at all.

Still, opportunity was beckoning. Maybe, down the line, I'd embrace it.

■ ■ ■

A few days after I did an interview on Aussie TV about New Orleans, Mtangulizi Sanyika, an old friend who is a veteran community organizer, sent me a short email asking if I would come to New Orleans to examine the dysfunctional recovery with an eye toward providing some informal advice. "MT," as I know him, explained that he had moved back to New Orleans to be with his ailing mother, and he was there when Katrina hit. He and I had a longstanding relationship from our days together at Berkeley, where I met him when I taught community development in one of my field labs. MT is an imposing figure: short, stocky, with a big, open face and a scraggly beard that refuses to become full. He always wears an African robe over his Western clothes and tops it off with a square, Middle Eastern, multicolored cap.

MT explained that before the storm he had formed an organization specifically to awaken New Orleans blacks to their rights and the need to alter the social and economic equations. We talked briefly on the telephone, and I agreed to make the long trip. I was going to Louisiana for a second time—again, at my own expense—to see what his group was doing, to see what New Orleans looked like a year after Katrina, and just out of curiosity. I recalled my dad's warning: "Curiosity killed the cat." Maybe so, I thought. But the temptation was great. And I had an interview about New Orleans coming up on a Sydney radio station, which set me to thinking more seriously about the post-Katrina situation.

I met MT at a New Orleans hotel in mid-November 2006. He took me for a ride around the city. I saw little moving. We went to the Ninth Ward, where houses had literally fallen into the street.

Next we visited Mtumishi St. Julien, director of the city's Housing Finance Authority, where a group of well-dressed, well-spoken African American men were arrayed around a table. The discussion centered on what these men could bring to the party, that is, the recovery programs to build housing or repair damaged city playgrounds. Together, they represented years of experience and talent, and they had financial resources. But although they were obviously able, there didn't appear to be a way to mobilize them. Discussions ensued on how to contact the city administration. No one had clear ideas. After the meeting I went to St. Julien's home, in the suburbs, to see the storm damage there.

I also met city council member Cynthia Willard-Lewis, a former state of Louisiana beauty queen with a strong resemblance to Lena Horne. As part of the recovery, she wanted buildings torn down by mayoral order because they had depressed property values and corroded public safety. I empathized with Willard-Lewis. The neighborhoods she represented had been disfigured by a monster dilapidated apartment building that never should have been built in that residential area. I said to her, "This shoddy high-rise along the freeway is simply poor city planning." She grunted in agreement and spoke at great length on how competently citizens in New Orleans East had started to re-plan the area before the storm hit.

Next day, we attended a series of forums and meetings on disaster plans. I left without learning either the goals of those organizations or their sponsors.

During the afternoon of my second day in New Orleans, the Rev. Louis Farrakhan, leader of the Nation of Islam, appeared at a church gathering. Several speakers told how most of the Katrina news reporting on looting, rape, and murder was not only erroneous but purposely distorted. Through descriptions of ordinary acts of heroism presented by eyewitnesses, such as individuals who took baby formula from stores or rubber swimming pools from hardware emporiums to float people out of harm's way, a truer picture emerged of what had occurred. The Superdome rapes didn't happen, according to several speakers at this forum. Moreover, local gangs in many cases acted as police while the small uniformed force of officers in that massive building were dealing with life and death emergencies. These facts were all news to me.

I met Farrakhan for a brief discussion on recovery approaches. I described the need to create jobs and develop economic resources early in the process. He was sympathetic but noncommittal about contributing to the recovery.

I joined a march through the public housing areas near downtown, which resounded with shouts and demands for social equity in rebuilding. Next day, a Sunday, I wandered the streets by myself and took more photos. I left the city for the airport with questions on my mind. Anticipating my queries, MT presented me with a gift of a load of books on Katrina, hot off the press, for airplane reading.

■ ■ ■

A couple of weeks later, I returned for a third time to New Orleans, to get a broader, more nuanced view of the city and its operational problems. My first two visits Stateside had confirmed that the city wasn't mobilizing itself—or perhaps wasn't able to mobilize its resources, both human and material—to move the recovery forward. Pre-Katrina tensions and problems were only exacerbated, and laid bare, after the storm.

On this third visit, I learned for the first time of the deep divisions and crises afflicting the city, especially around its competing plans for recovery. These divisions foreshadowed trouble for any recovery effort. My Urban Land Institute (ULI) colleagues, who had been so helpful in post-Rodney King Los Angeles, had made fissures in New Orleans. The ULI team that visited New Orleans was invited by Joe Canizaro, ULI's New Orleans-based president. A wealthy developer perceived to be a member of the upper elites, he was bringing in outsiders to re-plan the city. The resulting expert team report recommended that frequently flooded areas, mostly black and low-income communities, be abandoned and turned into park lands, as indicated by what would become infamous "green dots" on their map.

Although the report was careful to state that this could be done over time, and with minimum disruption, it provided for no meaningful community consultation. The whole effort was regarded by poor blacks and whites as another attempt to socially engineer them out of the city, a kind of geographic genocide.

The charge of a plot seemed even more plausible because just before Katrina, a large number of blacks had been evicted from their government-subsidized housing for so-called revitalization of those properties. By all accounts, most of the units were in good condition, their only liability being that they were close to downtown. The "green dot plan," as it came to be known, would be grabbed, black leaders charged, by outside real estate interests. Black renter populations would be displaced, and select parts of New Orleans turned into a white, Vegas-style gambling island.

I attended a series of workshops at one of the community centers in the city's central area. The workshop drew only a small audience, but the people in the room were a solid core of real community leaders. I presented the case for a consolidated plan for recovery with a coordinated approach with someone acting as the driving force—in effect, a recovery czar.

Odd as it may sound, I didn't have myself in mind for the job. Rather, I was thinking of Lieutenant General Russel Honoré, who had coordinated military relief efforts for Katrina-affected areas across the Gulf Coast. Honoré had already gained considerable recognition and respect for those actions. I hadn't any idea what a Pandora's box I was opening when I introduced the notion of a recovery czar.

On this visit I ordered business cards at a downtown printing establishment on St. Charles Avenue. When I went to pick up the cards, I hunted down a small café where I could get a sandwich. A group of white men were at a nearby table, talking loudly enough to be heard everywhere. I would hear the gist of their conversation repeated many times after I became recovery czar: the city was finally being rid of the low-income drag on the economy and would benefit if "they" didn't return. The group took no notice of me.

Those hostile remarks included a crude denunciation of the mayor that would become a norm. Except in movies, I hadn't heard anyone talk like that in a long time. I brought the subject up to MT. "Welcome to New Orleans," he said. "You have a lot to learn."

During this visit, MT arranged for a meeting with Mayor Nagin. Over breakfast on the morning of my meeting, I quickly sketched on a napkin an organizational chart for a recovery office that would operate under the mayor's authority.

The meeting began well. After chatting amicably, he asked my opinions of the city and the recovery underway. He also asked about my work in Australia and in post-earthquake and post-fire Oakland. Nagin knew something about me. He had done his homework, and his sincerity and integrity impressed me.

The mayor told me he wanted someone who had both experience with FEMA and knowledge of how a city worked to help him guide the complicated FEMA and state processes. He was not satisfied with his support staff, who seemed to him to know little more than he did about what to do and how to do it.

I had anticipated that MT would have turned my hand-sketched organizational chart into a finely typed and expertly drawn product. Instead, he handed me the napkin on which I had drawn the chart. The mayor peered at the napkin in his hand, pondered it, and then quizzed me on the plan and my whole approach to recovery. He stood up, which MT later confessed he took as a signal that the meeting had ended. But no: the mayor was standing to show me a large diagram near his desk. MT took a few photos of it. I told the mayor that I would be happy to help him as a consultant.

"No, I need you to come full time," he said.

I responded, "I'll see if that can be arranged."

Outside the office, I told MT that the mayor impressed me, and that he would be a great person to work with.

I knew then what was going to happen next. I was going to take the job.

But I had to have a good plan. On my visits, I'd already gotten useful intimations of the problems and issues that I knew would emerge and intensify once I was directing the recovery. And I was unsure how I could make things work in an atmosphere where there was so little mutual trust among the locals and, in Washington, so little confidence in the city and state administrations.

3. A HARBINGER OF PROBLEMS TO COME

I WENT BACK TO AUSTRALIA AND RETURNED A FEW WEEKS later, the first week of December 2006. I had asked the mayor to set up a meeting for me with the people I'd be working with, to see if there was some mutual comfort and a general agreement on what my role would be if I took the job.

I had a packed agenda. I met with police superintendent Warren Riley and chief administrative officer Brenda Hatfield, who said with a warm smile, "I'll be glad to get this recovery off my desk."

Legislative director and mayor's aide de camp Kenya Smith showed me around City Hall, and introduced me to city council members and staffers. I went to meet city attorney Penya Moses-Fields in her office. She told me that her role was to be the lawyer for the council and the city, and to be the mayor's and the city's conscience. I also met the mayor's communications chief, Ceeon Quiett.

In the evening, Mayor Nagin organized a dinner for me with the team. I met all the key people except Donna Addkison, chief of development.

Next day, when I did meet Addkison, it was an uncomfortable encounter. She is a small, energetic brunette, the epitome of professionalism, with bright eyes that beam at you like searchlights. I was taken aback when, throughout our interview, she played a television so loud that I had to ask her over and over again to repeat what she'd said. Even with those hints, she didn't turn off the TV or even lower the volume. She was also jumpy. She asked me my role and then, before I could answer, said that she had much of the recovery underway and that I wasn't needed.

Addkison invited to the meeting a man named she identified only as "Tony," one of her staff, a stoop-shouldered creole with curly hair and a solid build. I had no idea who he was or what he did. She didn't mention his title. But when the meeting ended, she said, "I know you want Tony on your staff. You can have him."

Walking me to the elevator, Tony apologized for the tenor of what had just occurred.

For my part, this was another harbinger of a potentially serious problem: I wasn't sure about joining the team if there might be holdouts. In disaster recovery, a senior holdout not only can hurt your program but can poison the work atmosphere. Although I wanted to meet with the mayor to discuss Addkison, I was only able to talk to him by phone just before I took the job. He assured me it would all work out. I had my doubts.

Council member Willard-Lewis was a vocal leader of the black community's recovery effort and set up meetings for me in the wards. I met for the first time with the full United New Orleans Plan (UNOP) senior team. Laurie Johnson and Steven Bingler were among its leaders.

As the UNOP team briefed me, it became clear that the city had a number of planning teams that were in competition with each other, including the controversial "green dots" plan I've described. They also gave me a briefing on the pre-Katrina population, which one said was a bit inflated since actual home occupancy levels based on water and gas meter use were much lower than the official census. I asked for their best guesses, which ranged from 385,000 to 454,000 but well short of the official 484,000 census figure of five years earlier. The lowest estimates were based on the dwellings drawing electricity and water regularly. As Greg Rigamer, the New Orleans economist/demographer, said, the number depends on what you want to count, those here all the time or those here some of the time. The city council commissioned neighborhood plans that it intended to present to the Louisiana Recovery Authority (LRA) as the city's recovery plan. In a hostile voice, I asked Laurie and Steve in the council chambers, "Why isn't this being done by the City Planning Office? This is the city's job."

Steve agreed calmly. "But Ed, you don't understand. The city doesn't have the capacity to *do* the job."

I would soon find out that he was right.

On this visit I also met with the New Orleans Redevelopment Authority, NORA. The first time I met the mayor, in early November 2006, I had made a simple request: if I take the job of recovery czar, then make me head of NORA, or at least put it under my direction. So far as I could tell, the agency had dealt none too successfully with blighted properties, and had no other real mandate.

The mayor liked my proposal, but informed me that NORA was a creature of the state, organized to do business in and for the city. That, I replied, was a strange arrangement, unless the agency received state money. I argued that he at least ought to have NORA report to me on the organization chart.

Again, Nagin agreed, but said, "Those guys are pretty independent. I'm not sure how they will take this idea."

"Those guys" meant principally NORA's board of directors—the president of Tulane University and other distinguished locals—and our problems with them would go beyond what the mayor had suggested in our conversation. In my first meeting with the board, I discovered that New Orleans's mayor couldn't and shouldn't assume he was going to lead the recovery from any disaster. NORA board members were already in the press and on radio and TV, outlining how they had a mandate from the mayor to lead the recovery.

From city government staff members and the few people I knew in New Orleans, I was more than a little concerned by what I was hearing about NORA's direction. The organization was publicly proclaiming that it was responsible for the recovery and that the mayor should just get out of the way.

How could I plan and carry out this massive reconstruction job if my boss and patron, mayor C. Ray Nagin, was going to be undercut by the very people who should be supporting us?

At my next meeting with Nagin and his policy executive counsel and policy advisor Becca O'Brien, about my proposed organizational structure for the task, I reemphasized my need to control NORA's strategy and funding program to ensure that the agency's role meshed efficiently with our recovery plan when we made one.

A significant disconnect in that regard was already clear. I just couldn't fathom how an independent development authority—called NORA or anything else—could have the power to do what it wanted with no city oversight or guidance. How could it be that a mayor appointed members of such a group to work on city projects, and they wound up acting independently of him?

The answer, it seemed to me, was rooted in political calculations on his part. The mayor wanted a group of stature to give him the capacity to make some fundamental changes in neighborhood commercial districts. He was both surprised and disturbed when NORA laid out an independent agenda not related to his goals. But having appointed them he had few options.

I had good reason for feeling that NORA ought to be under direct mayoral control, and that I was being directly challenged in my new position. I had written books and won awards for managing these kinds of recovery projects. Why would I now be up against what I considered an irrational organizational structure with the responsibility and power to do whatever it wanted in spite of the mayor, and in spite of me?

The mayor seemed to understand my frustration, and pledged his support to ensure that our operations ran smoothly. He smiled and added, "We got the money."

Fine, I thought, but who would run the recovery, and what would they be running?

My next encounter with NORA was on a return visit in early December 2006. I wanted to know what the members themselves thought their roles were and why they felt the need to be independent of the mayor and me. Becca arranged for the meeting in the mayor's office.

I had barely sat down and opened my notebook before invectives started flying at Nagin. Several members called him weak and ineffective, and said that he owed them—NORA—two million dollars. One member, a balding, bespectacled man, reddened and said, "We can get the recovery going if the mayor and city would just get out of the way. We have projects all lined up." I stayed silent and made notes as the meeting became extremely heated and hostile. More invective was unleashed, aimed generally at the city as well as specifically at Nagin.

Some of the phrasing, I had to admit, was colorful and stunningly direct. An ex-city council member described the mayor as nice but incompetent, a crawfish that promised one thing and then backed away as soon as anyone else objected. Another NORA board member, a short black man with flaring nostrils, called him a liar because he didn't provide NORA the money he promised. And a middle-aged white member declared that everybody knew "Ray" was a poor manager who didn't know how City Hall functioned—and even if he *did* know, he couldn't extract any work out of the civil service employees.

Then the NORA crew turned on me. I wouldn't get anything done, they said, because the mayor wouldn't support me, and, anyway, he wasn't in charge. They added that I didn't know anything about New Orleans.

I didn't even get a chance to introduce myself formally before Becca O'Brien adjourned the meeting.

She and I walked out, shaking our heads.

■　■　■

Although I had yet to join the Katrina recovery effort in an official, fulltime, paid capacity, I had already assimilated a vast amount of information from my visits to the United States and the city, and had drawn on all my past experience to start thinking about how I would run the operation, and the problems I'd encounter.

Early in this process, the mayor's assistant had sent me the city's priorities by email. The list was too long. I emailed back and said: "*This is not a priority list, this is a Christmas tree. Slim it down. Make it cleaner and more direct.*" So we made a shorter list, giving high priority to police, fire, and public safety projects.

The mayor and I decided to give the recovery more structure based on some principles we developed via email correspondence.

1. *Continue the healing.* Recognize that the underlying trauma of Katrina started well before the disaster, and lay in the deep divisions across race and class. Healing the chasms across the community is an ongoing exercise the Recovery Office has to play a central role in designing and carrying out. This process includes meetings of all city employees and community groups as an ongoing part of the recovery effort.

2. *Provide public safety and security to all neighborhoods.* The depth of fear of crime in the lowest-income communities is impeding the return of residents to them. But because crime is a citywide contagion affecting all areas, both crime prevention and crime stopping have to become critical elements of the recovery. The elements should include a host of programs such as citywide crime cameras and community and neighborhood policing strategies that engage young people in positive social and recreational pursuits.

   In addition, the availability of good schools near students' homes is an important security issue for every parent. Schools are now community core facilities. Libraries and community centers near schools increase foot traffic and reduce auto-oriented development, while increasing the viability of neighborhood retail. I felt that as energy became the key issue in the nation, New Orleans would be ideally suited as an attractive city to live and work in, if it could deal with climate change. Finally, good hospitals and clinics are required to deal with both mental and physical health issues. Therefore, a core element of the strategy is to provide every community with access to better health facilities than it had before Katrina.

A ruined house.
Author's photograph

3. *Install infrastructure for the twenty-first and twenty-second centuries.* New Orleans, like many American cities, has underinvested in primary infrastructure such as sewers and water. That is the bedrock for any new industries. It's important to all communities across all income groups, and it answers the needs of emerging enterprises for better, cheaper, and greener technologies.

4. *Diversify the economy.* The largest producers in the New Orleans economy, based as it is on tourism, energy, and retail services, are in low-wage service sectors. To combat crime and generate a healthy social economy, new job bases, related to the city's future, have to be established in areas such as biomedicine, advanced transportation, and media.

5. *Develop a sustainable settlement pattern.* This is the foundation of all good cities, whose viable neighborhoods attract people and jobs. Urban theorist Richard Florida, a good friend of mine, contends that attracting and retaining or educating highly educated young professionals is a smarter economic development approach than chasing factories. I wrote what some consider a seminal article on this same topic, applying the idea to a city economic development strategy. For me, the aim was to deepen the education and skills base of New

Orleans by working with the new school district to build new environmentally and socially sustainable communities, less segregated by income.

As I went around New Orleans during my four preliminary trips there, I had sensed despair, not hope. The formal and informal interviews I conducted only confirmed that impression.

I realized that New Orleans reminded me a great deal of my visits to some West African countries where I'd worked as a consultant several decades earlier. Although people knew that their countries contained resources, they had lost faith in their governments, and in the leaders who had plundered those resources. In New Orleans, as I listened to residents talk, I formed a picture of the storm ripping open a lot of old wounds—civic in the broad sense, but in many cases personal as well. So I realized that my work there would have to attack the core problems of the people, not just oversee a cosmetic recovery of buildings.

My vision of the situation was that the city was broken *before* the storm.

Those impressions were confirmed over and again by my conversations with local black leaders who were discouraged, and whites who were distrustful or antagonistic, most often toward each other. Old myths and deep grudges seemed to be thwarting the kind of cooperative behavior I'd experienced in Oakland and post-September 11 New York. In both those situations, I was swept up by an intense spirit of community collaboration and a desire to reaffirm a common destiny.

As a result, my operating philosophy as I contemplated the New Orleans assignment was to view it as akin to my earlier work in developing countries, where the restoration of good government and a clear economic order were more important than either the briefings I received from the World Bank and other agencies or the rhetoric of local community leaders.

New Orleans's economic destiny had to be changed. The city had become entirely dependent on tourism and soft-sector items like the sale of trinkets made overseas; it had few revenue producers except food, and almost no surviving national company headquarters. The oil bust had sent most of the major ones to Houston or Dallas.

So there was a one- (or at best two-) sided economy. I had to try to diversify that economy based on two factors: physical and human resources. New Orleans needed jobs that fit the skill levels of its people, which meant jobs requiring local labor with technical inputs. So driving forklifts and trucks, welding, and similar blue-collar jobs would be the goal. Expansion of the airport was a natural, especially given the needs of aircraft servicing. Jobs at a large logistics center, where goods were downloaded into containers and reconfigured or transshipped, also made sense.

My core challenge, as I saw it, would be to use the federal funds and private philanthropy that would be coming to New Orleans to build a team and an organizational structure that could reconstitute the city's basic institutions, including its economy and government. As in other disasters, my guiding idea was that the city should use the recovery process to improve its economy, government, housing, schools, and civic life for the future, and not just restore itself to what it was before—which in New Orleans's case, at least, was a dying and deteriorating city.

I'd start by leaning on my Oakland and New York experiences to use Katrina as the mechanism to change the city and give it a solid, new, and long-term direction. Part of that, maybe a large part, would involve major physical changes; in Oakland, we had extended Interstate 880 down to the busy port to move more goods faster as well as to restore the link between downtown and the oldest part of the city. That strategy also dovetailed with my goal of reinventing the downtown as a government, rather than retail, center.

I wanted to be clear about my thinking before I left for New Orleans in January 2007. I took a short vacation in Mexico from December 15, 2006, to January 6, 2007, and arrived with a little rest and lot of experience as well as a game plan based on what'd I'd seen there, and not with a template or a rigid theory to apply to every problem and situation. It never occurred to me to base the recovery schematically on what I'd done in Oakland, or helped to do in New York. I simply took pieces of my approach in those places, as well as all the other past work I'd done.

In my experience with disaster, it's best not to approach problems with a rigid template or philosophy, but to see what the situations present to you, and improvise. Like a lot of people, especially executives with sports backgrounds, I based my strategic thinking on sports leadership approaches. When I played quarterback in high school and college, I always took what the defense "gave" me, as football coaches put it. My game plan was to play to the opposition's weakness until the defense stopped us. If the other team was big and fast, I slowed the game down and frustrated them with dinky passes and "screen" passes. If they were smart, I let them lead until I saw their strategy— and then countered it. I didn't take plays from coaches or anybody else on the sideline unless I felt I had to.

In New Orleans, I found myself utilizing that quarterbacking philosophy of taking what the defense will give you. I had a general game plan, but I figured on letting it evolve as the political, economic and social situations revealed themselves in more detail. As my UC-Riverside coach Jim Whittley drummed into me, study the defense and let the other team make mistakes, and know them on film better than they know you. Don't try to overwhelm them, let them beat themselves.

Although the post-Katrina assignment was inevitably somewhat daunting, I felt that my skills as an economic and international development planner gave me some chance for success. I knew, however, I would need a lot of luck and courage to go the distance.

In post-Katrina New Orleans, I figured getting down the field was the goal. It would take a long time to record victories. We needed to deal with internal strife among members of the community on race, class, and a myriad other agendas before we could move forward anywhere.

Since I had visited New Orleans four times before taking the job of the recovery czar, and each time took back volumes of records about the hurricane and the attempts to resurrect the city, I designed a recovery system based on what I had gleaned and learned from these trips and from previous disasters I'd been involved in. I didn't want—or need—to reinvent the wheel, and I responded to what the situation presented to me. I also had the advantage of advice from university colleagues from Los Angeles; Kobe, Japan; and the World Bank.

■　■　■

After the last visit in December 2006, I communicated with Mayor Nagin by email from my home in Australia and later on vacation in Mexico. I liked him and wanted to be part of his team. So I told him I was coming to New Orleans, but not when. First I had to disengage from the university and discuss several problematic issues with Maaike. I was more than a little nervous about being away at that juncture. I was on my way to Australian citizenship, which is stringent with respect to residency. One can lose a permanent visa, much like a U.S. "green card," by staying outside the country too long.

The University of Sydney indicated that it might give me a one-year leave if I could pay for a teaching replacement and for my research staff salaries, and if by using Skype and email I could also continue working on my research grants and doctoral student supervision. The mayor found a formula that worked for the university and for New Orleans. My wife agreed that I could go if I made it a one-year commitment, subject to her approval for an extended year, and if I could keep my Australian permanent visa. She and had I just purchased a house we liked, and she was staying behind to furnish it.

I finally got everything done with the university and family. Then I pressed the mayor for a title and responsibilities that would give me authority over all recovery operations. My sojourns in New Orleans had convinced me that there were already too many players ready to seize the reins of the recovery, including insiders like Addkison and outsiders like the NORA Board and its new staff members. Furthermore, the city council was developing its own recovery plans, and there were competing plans afoot. So I felt I had to be designated at least deputy mayor or deputy to the mayor for recovery.

Since Nagin and I couldn't agree by way of email, I was hoping that my face-to-face meeting in early December 2006 would get our respective expectations sorted out. The idea of a major domo with power over the rest of the bureaucracy of the type I was proposing clearly troubled him. He wrote to say that the team was set and that he didn't want to upset the current working arrangements by bringing in someone who appeared to have authority superior to that of the other managers.

I agreed to a point. But I told him that my experience in Oakland showed that if people aren't clear on what orders to follow, they'll cling to the old organizational structure, slowing things down. I felt that my experience with Addkison hinted that the same thing might happen in New Orleans.

We left the matter of my specific title for later. Meanwhile, I came up with "Executive Director of Recovery Management" as the proxy title for use in the city council budget, with discussion to follow on what it meant.

We shouldn't have had to discuss this further. We were already nearly 15 months beyond the storm.

I WAS ANNOUNCED AS THE RECOVERY "CZAR" IN NEW Orleans on January 7, 2007, 16 months after Katrina. "Dr. Blakely, a globe-trotting academic with a long résumé, has a mandate for renewal from Mayor C. Ray Nagin and a city desperate for leadership," reported the *New York Times* on my appointment.

Even with my experiences with major disasters in Oakland, Los Angeles, and New York; even with my extensive nonacademic resume; even with my successes in the nonprofit sector working with large staffs and budgets; even with my international experiences in unfamiliar cultures ranging from Turkey to the Caribbean to West Africa; and even with a 1988 run for the mayor of Oakland under my belt and plenty of experience working with mayors directly, I realized one thing quickly: New Orleans presented a far greater challenge than anywhere else I'd been.

Rumors of my appointment were already afloat in the media, and in an early December 2006 press gathering at a community center, I had commented on what I might do if appointed. But the mayor and I didn't reach an agreement on the appointment until mid-December, after I had secured leave from the University of Sydney, and my agreement with New Orleans was verbal, with no written contract, and no job description to speak of. The only thing I had from mayor Nagin was his injunction: "Fix It!"

What the hell did *that* mean? I'd heard "fix it!" before—from mayor Lionel Wilson of Oakland after the 1989 earthquake, and from his successor, Elihu Harris, two years later, after the Oakland Hills fires. Hearing it again set off warnings for me about the kinds of political issues I might face from citizens and the support or lack thereof I might expect from the mayor and his team.

The ride downtown from the airport that January day was like passing through one long, uninterrupted place of mourning. Sand seemed to cover every surface. The skies, along with everything else, were dull gray. I saw no birds flying or roosting. Along the freeway and tucked under the overpasses vehicles lay rusting, right where they had been deposited by the storm or abandoned by their owners. I saw blue roofs and debris stacked in cul-de-sacs that abutted the freeway. Perhaps worst of all, the stench of dead animals, still lying in the open, periodically assaulted my nostrils. The entire scene was almost as nauseating as it was eerie—and this was fully 16 months after Katrina made landfall.

Waiting at the airport for my contact, Becca O'Brien, I was struck by the greetings and reunions I observed around me. As the local folk met travelers, smiles and expressions of pleasure were notably absent. People hugged and cried. They whispered to one another as if at a funeral. The terminal offered no relief. The waiting areas, ticket counters, and baggage claims were dark, drab, and cold. The place looked and smelled like a morgue.

Becca gave me a cordial hello, put me into her city SUV, and we took off. No traffic slowed our journey; indeed, I saw little moving. Downtown wasn't much better. When we passed City Hall, a massive and dismal Soviet-style building, I glanced at the electric sign and saw that it was broken. "C..t Y H..L ...," the sign said. I wondered why no one had turned it off. In front was a park of sorts, an unkempt grassy knoll with few benches or any other gracious touches of a public space.

As we approached the massive Superdome, where reconstruction operations *were* underway, we had to dodge potholes and twisted trees on a sandy Poydras Street, one of the city's main thoroughfares. And Poydras, as a central artery, had been cleared more than other streets. The nearby city library looked grim and unwelcoming. The signs of various service agencies hung from it. In every other respect, it appeared lifeless.

Our vehicle came to a stop at the Pavilion Hotel, a great remnant of a past era of Florentine architecture in New Orleans. I prepared for an early bedtime, to counter the Oakland-to-New Orleans time change, and after a surprisingly sound sleep, I hit the hotel gym. It was 5:30 a.m., so I had the place to myself. Then I walked a couple of blocks in the brightening early morning. At first, I couldn't figure out what was strange before I realized, again, that there were no birds.

Then it was time to meet the mayor and his legislative and intergovernmental affairs assistant, Kenya Smith. We needed to go over the press release that would announce my appointment as the recovery czar. Donning the red tie my wife thought suitable for this occasion, I descended to the Pavilion's dining room and was ushered to the mayor's reserved table in the far right corner. Mayor C. Ray Nagin came into the room with the smooth gait of a basketball player, and with Kenya at his side. A light-skinned African American with a strong face, Nagin calls to mind a pro athlete you've seen before, but can't match the name with the face. He looked tall and cool, in a well-fitting dark suit. His bald head was gleaming, and he had a smile on his lips. He glided over to his table like he was walking on water. Plain-clothes security men hovered at a respectful but watchful distance.

The three of us chatted a short while before the mayor asked, "You ready?"

I had expected to get a full briefing that would clarify my role and title, which were still under discussion. None of those items were discussed, however, even when I suggested that we do so. I wanted more detail from the mayor, as well as a personal exchange, but that wasn't possible in front of an aide. And now we were taking off for City Hall and the press conference.

Reporters, photographers, and cameramen were gathered in what is today called the City Hall "media room." Nagin called them to attention, smoothed out a long piece of paper, and started to introduce me as the head of the recovery. Almost immediately, the reporters pounced:

Why so long in getting someone to do this? Why do you need anyone?

Mayor announces me.
Author's photograph

Aren't you the mayor? Can't you or your staff do the job? Who will he report to? Why *this* guy? What does he know about New Orleans? How much is he getting paid? What's he going to do, and how fast will he do it?

These were far from friendly, or even neutral, questions. And I was pretty ill-prepared to answer most of them. Although I had an extensive disaster recovery resume and was "in command," at this point I had only a superficial understanding of what being there, or being in command, would mean. I had no real understanding of my job—nor any pre-briefing or script for the interview. In my past positions, in contrast, encounters like this were always rehearsed.

The reporters started in on me. Why were you hired? What staff will you have? What's going to be different with you here? Why do you think you can move this recovery along when no one else has?

Feeling suddenly flushed and combative, I shot back that I would have a plan of action and funding for the plan by the end of the year.

That wasn't good enough. Again the question came—what difference are you going to make?

I responded hotly: "That's not a question. It's a challenge. Come back in a year."

I looked over at the mayor. His ears seemed to shoot up. His media director called the press conference to an end. But, for me, it was a start, and a rough and irritating one, at that.

Nagin, media advisor Ceeon Quiett, Kenya, Becca, and I all walked back to the mayor's office. Nagin took his seat at the head of a long, oval mahogany table with matching black leatherette arm chairs.

"Are they always like that?" I asked.

The mayor's left eyebrow went up in mock horror. "Man," he replied, "have you ever met a press corps like that?"

"*No!*" I said in a firm radio voice.

"Well, you haven't seen anything yet," the media director said quickly.

Nagin grinned. "You'll learn." He giggled uncontrollably and shook his head from side to side like a schoolboy telling a dirty joke.

The media director said, "We have media lined up for Becca and Blakely today." Then he started speaking in media code about radio and TV stations. I tuned out.

We jumped into another SUV and tore down the street, and Becca again recited the Katrina tragedy for me. She was making sure I was on message.

As I hurriedly rehearsed my list of facts, our SUV came to an abrupt halt.

We jumped out and bounded into the first radio station studio, along with some young and funky rap disc jockeys who were more interested in their street banter with one another than in us.

When we left the third and last radio station I went to find a home at City Hall. I sat down at a small desk in a vacant office, which I simply commandeered. No one offered to help me or show me around. I thought about how I got here, what I was going to do. I wandered around the offices and poked my head into them. One of my first new hires, my environmental specialist, was already at work before I could even get a contract organized for her. What dedication!

I made an arrangement for a city vehicle—simply by taking the first small black or blue car available—and tried to fill in the prescribed paperwork.

Before I knew it, my first day was over.

I walked out of the office and into the hallway. My new police escort and driver, Roland Doucette, or Duce, as he told me he likes to be called, was waiting for me. Duce is my height, weight, and coloring. We wear mustaches—his pencil and mine bushy. He cuts his hair close so it looks almost like a cap on his head. He is well built, and when he stands with his legs out, you know he's a cop. He is surely someone you don't want to mess with.

Duce asked simply, "You ready?" and we walked out the back door and got into his silver Ford Taurus. It looked like a police vehicle without a decal.

I'd rented the apartment of an old friend, in the central area near downtown. When we got to the flat we lugged my suitcases up the steps.

As Duce was going down the stairs, he yelled back, "Doc, you got mail."

I called back, "What? I haven't even told the mayor where I'm living."

As I reached the bottom landing and Duce handed me the parcel, he replied, his eyes wide and piercing, "This is a small town, Doc, don't you forget it."

To be away from the street noise, I took the back bedroom in my two-bedroom flat, arranged my clothes in the closet, and then went into the kitchen to look for food. I hadn't been invited for dinner on my first night by any of my colleagues nor by the mayor. So much for Southern hospitality, I thought. I didn't realize at the time that during my two years in New Orleans I would never get an invitation to dinner because so many people's homes and lives were deeply disrupted.

That struck me as strange, even in a crisis. The mayor and most of his lieutenants had impressed me with their MBAs and professional degrees when I met them. But to my mind, one of the cardinal rules of a manager is to welcome all new staff with dinner or lunch. I'd acted on that rule for more than forty years and had it drilled home at the Pacific Telephone Company, my first post-college employer, and as an Air Force officer. Yet here, in New Orleans, no one even asked me if I had a place to stay. This was not bad manners, just a very bad situation for everyone.

As I walked down St. Charles Avenue in search of dinner, a large black rat was sauntering across the street and moving toward the downed power lines on my side. I hoped for a second the lines were live, so they would fry the vermin. But the rat eased across them and up some steps toward a house. He'd had the place to himself for so long that I was the interloper.

Back in the apartment, I took off my clothes, put on a sweat suit, and opened a can of beans and a packet of rice. I found suitable kitchen utensils and started the fire. For more than 50 years, I've made evening and weekend field notes. I took out my notebook and small ballpoint pen and began writing:

To Be Fixed
1. Who is responsible for this recovery?
2. What is the recovery plan?
   - Where is the city master plan? Why isn't the planning commission developing and driving the recovery process as part of a long-term master plan?
3. What are the city's recovery priorities?
   - There are no management systems to run the city or manage the recovery.
   - Jails and criminal justice facilities are an admission of failure, not priorities for a better city
   - Infrastructure is a mess—old or broken
   - How can you have a real city without good schools—they are not even mentioned
   - Blight is a visible issue
4. What is the city economic base—oil? tourism?
5. Can we fashion a city bureaucracy to guide the recovery?
6. What is FEMA doing to help restore New Orleans?
7. Race is an apparent issue
8. Can New Orleans fool Mother Nature?

—A beginning list!

PART II

Where to from Here?

MAYOR NAGIN WAS ON THE HORNS OF A DILEMMA. HE HAD to decide among at least three competing recovery plans: one promoted by the Bring New Orleans Back (BNOB) commission; the second, a scheme of neighborhood plans put forward by the consulting firm of Lambert and Associates; and the third, an initiative by the Greater New Orleans Foundation (GNOF) to synthesize all the plans from all over the city into one consolidated monster plan covering everything the city ever needed or wanted.

BNOB was developed primarily by the business community with the mayor's agreement. It used soon-to-be-infamous "green dots" to represent vast tracts of land that had been repeatedly flooded. The BNOB and its advisory team, to recall, had proposed that these areas not be rebuilt, but instead should be converted to parks or other uses. The BNOB team recognized that the extreme post-Katrina abandonment would force city residents to move to higher ground and repopulate the central areas. Although that was logical in terms of land use and economic development, the green dot areas targeted for conversion appeared largely on low-income, predominantly black areas of the city where homeownership was high. As a result, a lot of black-owned properties would be sacrificed. The black community thus characterized BNOB as a "whitey land grab," and it seemed that Mayor Nagin's hand-picked group had sanctioned that solution.

The city council, with President Oliver Thomas and other African American members taking the lead, reacted to BNOB. They employed Lambert and Associates to develop a neighborhood-based recovery that preserved the essence of all neighborhoods. Lambert's approach was based on old boundaries and had been assembled hastily to foil any attempt to use the BNOB plan. I discovered on one of my trips with my friend MT that African American community leaders were nervous about the competing plans because the BNOB group—the "shadows," as MT and black leaders called the local establishment and its mouthpiece, the *Times-Picayune*—were always inserting themselves into various processes to establish the BNOB approach or some semblance of it as the official plan for New Orleans. The result would be a smaller black population.

To resolve the mounting competition and the escalating racial tensions over plans, the GNOF proposed to use its good offices as a neutral party to merge all the proposals into a unified, overarching document that would serve as the basis for a new, citywide master plan. The Rockefeller Foundation got involved behind the GNOF plan. Searching for a way to serve the city in this crisis, the Foundation discerned enough interest from the mayor and others to try to forge a final, unified effort, and the GNOF's offer seemed to be the best way to proceed. The vehicle for the plan (in keeping with the alphabet soup of the entire recovery) was the Unified New Orleans Plan, UNOP.

Unfortunately, some black civic leaders viewed this approach as nothing more than a back-door reimposition of the BNOB plan. Some BNOB volunteers were also involved in the UNOP process. Moreover, the mayor, although distancing himself from the green dots and many other aspects of the BNOB plan, said publicly that he wanted parts of BNOB incorporated into UNOP.

In addition to being a plan, UNOP was an enormous project to reach out to the New Orleans diasporas. The Greater New Orleans Foundation spent millions from the Rockefeller grant to hold civic forums, not only at large gatherings around the city but also at key locations around the nation by way of video conferencing and live videocasting. Rockefeller had paid America Speaks to help facilitate a similar process for New York's Ground Zero recovery plans. America Speaks tries to find common themes and threads to help professional planners and decision makers forge a workable agreement.

To increase the chances of success, Rockefeller temporarily posted two of its people to the GNOF staff. The UNOP program was sizable. It went well beyond the physical recovery of the city to embrace social, educational, and other longstanding civic issues, with most of the attention paid to non-city government concerns such as schools. It was a good summary of needs but not really a plan.

■　■　■

My task was to build something useful and usable from all the plan submissions, and to implement the UNOP goals onto the "map" of New Orleans, based on dynamics of urban growth. This meant finding the good ideas in a crowded, hard-to-navigate field that contained many good approaches but no central theme.

Before I arrived in New Orleans, I'd already started the planning work in earnest. I drew on my earlier disaster experiences to create a recovery blueprint. I had copies of all the plans, and I knew the federal rules governing them. Poring over the documents, I could see remarkable similarities in the places and projects recommended.

I was drawing on my previous experiences as a consultant and key leader on large-scale plans in Australia, China, and Korea, as well as, most recently, vice chair of the board of the Presidio in San Francisco, a decommissioned 1,200-acre former military base, the size and complexity of a city within the City of San Francisco's borders. Essentially, post-storm New Orleans was a large-scale metropolitan planning opportunity. So I approached the effort not as a disaster, but as the redevelopment of a large area much like the Presidio, in fact—and like Pudong (near Shanghai) and Australian projects where we planned or replanned thousands of acres of land with all the components from housing to transportation to economic development.

In this respect, UNOP data were invaluable to me, as the project amounted to background information from which one might set priorities for a recovery. As I read and tried to digest these plans, it became clear that I could actually strike a balance between the social and economic issues and the need to devise a land use plan.

Alongside the documents, I laid the template for regional planning that I'd developed over many years of teaching and included in various forms in my books and articles. This is what I devised as a list of essentials:

1. Establishing natural development patterns so transportation and land uses easily intersect—in essence, going with the land flow to facilitate the intersections between transport, housing, and commercial uses.
2. Identifying magnet infrastructure, meaning a combination of natural and institutional resources that can drive the regional and local economy. My usual metaphor of magnet infrastructure is the San Francisco Bay Area, with its great climate, demographic diversity, cultural richness, and its incomparable scientific research bases with UC-Berkeley, the UC Medical Campus, and Stanford.

3. Developing a clear identity for the place, making sure that the identity is distinctive and not just "me too." In New Orleans, this would not be easy: the physical identity of a trade and transport hub had eroded, and the popular image of music and creativity was being undercut by Memphis and other music hubs. In addition, New Orleans was becoming known more for sleaze than for good entertainment.

4. Establishing an economic engine that is globally competitive but locally based—much as in Pittsburgh, for example, where the loss of the steel mills was softened by a transition to a globally competitive, export-oriented technology base.

5. Creating the intersection between arts, culture, and education to attract human resources in a combination that few other places possess. Here I usually cite Seattle and Minneapolis as illustrative of deeply creative cultures that, in those cities, support Microsoft and 3M.

6. Establishing a policy body as a collaborative reference group to champion and push forward a regional plan and agenda (in this case the collective city rebuilding plan) separate from government. Examples include the Regional Plan Association in New York, and Joint Venture-Silicon Valley. I had helped form such organizations in several places, most recently on Long Island (the Long Island Index). In New Orleans, it was the Parish Recovery Council.

My approach would be to provide a set of priorities for public buildings, combined with geographically specific and defined economic recovery directions. As such, the approach would meet FEMA's requirements to release federal disaster funds.

Even while still home in Sydney, I had used Google Earth maps to examine the terrain, housing patterns, and commercial areas, along with demographic data my research staff at the University of Sydney developed. I found neighborhoods that, because of their strategic location and elevation, could revive faster than the rest of the city. These recovery areas were identified in various ways by the UNOP and other plans. I called them, in planner-speak, "key nodes." Playing around with them, I first identified five or six, then ten, and eventually sixteen.

After I was on the job in New Orleans and had selected my new director for planning and infrastructure, Dubravka Gilic, I asked her to give me an independent assessment of locales in which she would choose to launch a recovery based on the UNOP plan. Gilic had worked for many years on the Planning Commission, so she knew the most logical growth nodes in the city.

She and I agreed that thirteen of the sixteen nodes should be given highest priority in terms of resources and attention. The hurricane had hit the Ninth Ward hardest, so the Ninth became the poster child for Katrina destruction. It made sense to designate more than one target area there—the Holy Cross neighborhood and the *lower* Ninth. Dubravka had left out the Vietnamese section in the far eastern part of the city, and I added that. I also added Bywater. She omitted it because she thought it too small and relatively undamaged. But Bywater is well known for its art institutions, and I felt it was important to get them up and running as soon as possible.

My team took two months to craft the recovery approach that we dubbed the Target Area Plan. I give every project a name or label. In fact, I can't work on an idea until I have a label for communicating it. (For example, in Melbourne I had invented "technology precinct" to describe a scheme for concentrated university technology spinoffs; and in Brisbane I used a "gateway strategy" to describe an economic development program to reinforce the notion that Brisbane is the gateway to Asia.)

The point of the target areas designation was to have a visible operations metaphor that people could understand as the direction for the recovery. I invented this concept to designate areas for priority attention that combined residential improvement and commercial revitalization in the same locations. I presented these areas as the places to start a recovery that could, from there, radiate outward across the city. My rationale was that we didn't have enough money to do everything at once. If we could get started on strategic high ground, then residential development would increase in these areas and this in turn would support local businesses. I was also interested in some of the target areas, such as the Mississippi River areas and central downtown, as places to kick-start the economy.

Getting started early and in tangible ways is also important as a general principle. I knew from my disaster experiences in Oakland that you had to start quickly and with key places and projects as you worked toward the broader goals. People want to see *physical things*, and the things they see early need to be precursors to what comes later, so you can show what you're doing while you're doing it. I reminded Mayor Nagin that there *is* no recovery for ordinary people if they don't see stuff happening on or near their street.

With the Target Area Plan, rather than think in terms of reconstruction of pre-storm conditions, I invented three descriptive categories of work for the target areas: *rebuild, redevelop,* and *renew.* Rebuild applied to areas so devastated that you had to start from the bottom and redo everything; redevelop designated important pre-storm sections that suffered medium damage that could be addressed by a traditional redevelopment agency; and renew described areas so lightly touched that a small stimulus on our part would quickly produce private sector investments.

We asked NORA to use these places as its development focus by acquiring the dilapidated residential and commercial properties in the target areas. A matrix on our website described them in more detail; see Table 1.

My office—the Office of Recovery Management (ORM)—was initially strictly designed to plan, with no implementation capacities. So we aimed at the neighborhood level in a recognizable and sustainable pattern that used city resources and community centers as anchors. We knew some areas would come back on their own, because they had suffered almost no storm damage and had considerable wealth and a thriving, prestorm commercial base. Examples included the French Quarter and the Uptown areas close to the Mississippi River's earthen levees.

The viability of areas slow to recover hinged on a combination of factors: insurance issues, expense and complexity of construction, uncertainty about health care, education, and other services, and lingering concerns about protection from future storms. In all target areas, there was—and remains—a

TABLE 1

Rebuild	An area that has experienced severe destruction of its physical structures and social networks. The area will require major rebuilding and significant public and private investment for its recovery. With investment, it should have a high potential to attract investment and act as a catalyst for further redevelopment and recovery of the affected community.
Redevelop	An area of major redevelopment where key recovery strategies can be demonstrated. Some recovery components and resources are already present. This type of area also has a high potential for attracting investment and for acting as a catalyst for further community redevelopment and recovery.
Renew	An area or a specific project that requires relatively modest public intervention (resources and/or administrative action) that will add to the renewal and supplementary work as well as investment of the private and nonprofit sector already vested in the area. By combining and leveraging multiple resources, these projects provide a great return on public investment.

persistent "first-mover" disadvantage. Few people want to be the first to return to a neighborhood without residents or services. Property owners want to know that an investment in rebuilding will give them a home and help give them a community. However, if everyone waits for someone else to start, neighborhoods will languish and the recovery will stall. So in these areas we initiated small projects—neighborhood markets, community centers, and parks—as soon as we could.

The UNOP planners understood the benefits of focused development, and included the idea in an approach called Neighborhood Stabilization, or "clustering." The idea of clusters has a long history in urban design. Although first proposed in the 1960s to fight sprawl and protect open space, they are as old as the city itself. In fact, most cities naturally evolve in a cluster pattern, beginning with small, dense areas and growing outward. New Orleans is a classic example. It started in the French Quarter and grew to Tremé, in the heart of the city.

My staff, the UNOP team, and I all agreed that city government was the ideal entity for bringing cluster developments into being, not only as a coordinator but also as a partner in the development process. A city can use its assets (for example, schools, parks, libraries, recreation centers, and police stations) to give each cluster, or target area, the economic and social base it needs to get started.

■ ■ ■

For all its virtues, I knew that our Target Area Plan might tread on many toes. So my staff and I designed a strategy to promote its acceptance. We first vetted it with the city planning notables I'd met in Shreveport to see if they concurred that the idea was politically sound. Then I organized staff in teams of two to call on community-based organizations in the proposed target areas.

Just as with any product, we needed early adopters, or "clients." We sought them in the places that had the most to gain from our approach. Then I met with the UNOP and Lambert teams, so they could see that their work had become an integral part of our process. I also talked with each council member and his or her staff to get their comments on whether the plan met the spirit and the goals of the recovery program.

The target area approach was well received, and it served as the basis for the recovery effort. "It's promising to see somebody who is giving us a program that's based on a realistic assessment of potential resources," said Janet Howard, president of the Bureau of Governmental Research.

National and local media acknowledged the 17-point plan with the addition of a target area for Algiers (up from 16 original locations) as a good way to articulate the citywide recovery strategy. The keys to its success as a plan were to set and meet criteria for recovery and sustainability, and to bundle projects. National newspapers reported that "'[Blakely] has brought a level of realism to rebuilding New Orleans that hasn't been there,' said Sean Reilly, a member of the Louisiana Recovery Authority. 'He's got a real, concrete plan. At the end of the day, that's what's been missing: that clear prioritization, [a conviction that] here's where we're going to invest.'"

Yet support from the media, council members, and other community leaders as clients wasn't enough on its own. I also needed to communicate and promote the target area approach with New Orleanians themselves. I knew from the recovery in Oakland that out in the community, as opposed to meetings of professionals, "plans" are not understood unless you explain to ordinary folk how they're to be implemented. Plans need a face, and tangible explanations. I also knew how essential it was that I be visible and personally deliver my message.

To communicate the basic idea of the recovery plan, I used a bicycle.

In many other places, I'd climbed on my bike and pedaled around town, often with members of my staff. I first got the idea from Allan Jacobs, a famous street planner and a colleague at UC-Berkeley. Allan ran a class on how to read neighborhoods by walking through them. I went on walks with him until I honed the approach for use in my own classes, and in my disaster recovery work. When I was off the bike I was working with some of the many thousands of young and not so young volunteers who came to make a difference in New Orleans and to somehow make a difference in their own lives. Most weekends my volunteer coordinator had somewhere I had to go to and work as well as inspire the people doing the work. Much of the work, like gutting buildings or pulling weeds, was very hard on the people who did it physically, and when they saw so little change in the place it was a bit daunting psychologically. Getting volunteers to do work we needed versus what they wanted to do was difficult. Moreover, the real volunteer help we needed was to do the leg work of counting houses for our neighborhood house-by-house database and computer analysis to guide our various recovery programs, ranging from deciding on demolitions to targeting lending programs. While I appreciated all the energy, it cost the city a lot of time and money simply to go around and pick up the debris they generated and to ensure their safety. City and Sheriff's Office staff gave up their time on weekends too to assist and protect the volunteers.

Through close observation I can discern a neighborhood's history, social conditions, and economic transformations over fifty years, or longer. I liked to use this method to inform myself on how communities in a city operate socially and economically over time. By looking at trees, porches, and additions to houses, I can tell which ethnic groups occupied an area, from its founding to the present. I also teach this approach to my urban planning students.

For my classes at USC, we used bikes for this close observation, as they were more convenient than walking.

My first significant purchase in New Orleans was a bike. In January 2007, my second week on the job, I started pedaling around my own neighborhood first. I saw that my neighborhood needed street repairs, but instead got curbside attention from the neighbors working to keep their place clean and attractive.

Before long people began to join me on my bike expeditions. In late February, after Mardi Gras, I asked city council members to set up bike tours in their areas on Saturday mornings. I had no idea whether the media would be interested in these forays—or whether residents of neighborhoods other than my own would come along. But after the third excursion, they were a fixture for the media and a device for me to see up close both storm damage and pre-storm problems, and to craft more fine-grained approaches to dealing with them. Serendipitously, the bicycle rides also gave me "street cred" with many communities.

Soon enough I became known as "the Bicycle Guy." New Orleans is a bike-friendly city. Many people bike to work, and weekends are family cycling days. I tapped into a community culture by doing my bicycling on Saturdays, when parents and kids could come along. Riding on the weekends also allowed council members to join me, which stimulated dialogue with citizens of the neighborhoods they represented. Because not everyone could or would ride a bike, we held large "stationary" meetings at the conclusions of the rides, with a city council member acting as moderator.

I took along not only my staff but also 32 students from MIT and UCLA and some from Harvard. Going house to house and surveying damage, the students created additional visibility for the target area concept.

As I rode through a community, I could observe not only physical characteristics but also how people interacted with one another on the street, what they took care of, and what they allowed to fall into disrepair. I got to know many neighborhoods on my bike tours.

It also became clear to me through these trips that in some areas the damage happened less from Katrina—water or wind—than from previous neglect. Any urban planner, including me, can quickly distinguish between neglect and water damage. FEMA also appreciated the difference, and the agency heavily discounted projects if evaluations consistently cited a lack of maintenance.

City staff and local residents couldn't understand that approach. They took the position that Corps of Engineer levees, not neglect, had destroyed the city. Everything, they reasoned, could and should be restored to a new, higher quality. Residents told me, "If the thing fell down, they should give us one hundred percent for it."

FEMA, on the other hand, often maintained that before the storm the structure was *already* falling down. The agency said it shouldn't give the city any money for an unusable building or part of one that hadn't been used. While I didn't like the FEMA approach, I understood it. After all, the basic thrust of the FEMA legislation was to repair to the prior condition and no more. That keeps communities from getting newer facilities after a disaster than those they had before it, at taxpayer expense.

I also needed ways to build support and enthusiasm for the Target Area Plan among city employees. To accomplish this goal I drew on my five years as an executive with Pacific Telephone. During that time, I was responsible for installing telephones in one of the fastest-growing regions of the nation, Southern California's San Gabriel Valley, which runs from Pasadena in the east to the San Fernando Valley in the west. My job was to make sure that new wiring and installation equipment were delivered on time and to get our customers in the homes we wired to buy more telephone equipment and use the wiring Pac Bell was putting in. We anticipated the computer revolution and put in far more wiring in every home than a single telephone required.

To make this pay, the company sold customers on the idea of telephone equipment for every room in the house. In 1960, this was novel.

We knew that the best salespeople to sell telephone equipment were our telephone installers themselves. We also knew, from research conducted by our marketing firm, that if the installers didn't like the product, no inducement would get them to sell it. So my job was to get our staff, at every level in my division, to buy new company products ranging from small bedside phones to elaborate multitasking handsets with "hold" features and other conveniences. Pacific Telephone was the biggest private employer in the state of California, so our employee word-of-mouth sales force was a large and powerful one.

When I started working with Lionel Wilson, the three-time mayor of Oakland from 1978 to 1990, I applied the same approach to many policy areas. Wilson and I knew that every one of our city employees came in contact with at least ten residents. We therefore aimed materials at them via our internal television and newsletters as one way to promote complex ideas such as new bond issues for city libraries. Oakland's city manager, Henry Gardner, had a master's degree in administration. He was well acquainted with this approach, and he embraced it. After the earthquake and fire, Gardner and I developed a series of strategies to inform city staff and get them on board.

I coupled these approaches with staff development sessions on new city strategies. I led most of these sessions or had a hand in organizing them.

It occurred to me to design this same kind of program to sell the Target Area Plan to our own city employees. I used America Speaks, with its formulas and expertise, to solicit employee input on how they might contribute to the recovery and set priorities for their own agencies, as individuals, and for the city as a whole. The Rockefeller Foundation saw this as a natural follow-up on public needs and aspirations. So I had staff develop the UNOP priorities and compare them with those of the entire community. That allowed me to introduce the target area concept as one way of fitting community needs into a delivery formula that the staff could carry out.

We mixed staff members from various agencies at tables of ten, and gave them imaginary resources and a fictitious target area that would be suitable for one of our three approaches (rebuild, redevelop, or renew). The goal was to see if the resources helped solve the problems and, if not, to devise another solution that would make good use of our resources.

To make the exercise work, and to simulate cross-bureaucracy collaboration, we allowed the tables to trade resources. In the evaluations we received, staff liked the ideas and the goals, but felt that the current bureaucracy couldn't perform to recovery expectations or accommodate such broad collaborations. The evaluators felt there were too many barriers and no incentives to do things a different way. Alas, that judgment was correct.

The Target Area Plan coalesced out of all the processes I've described. It not only built on the work of the community, but also justified that work in concrete terms. The plan went on to become the catalyst for a great deal of civic action in New Orleans during 2007, the first year of my tenure there. Considering the intense controversy, suspicion, and criticism around competing recovery plans before my arrival in New Orleans, it's remarkable that the Target Area Plan generated no notable public complaints or disputes. The target areas have become the new community drivers and rallying points for the post-Katrina recovery. For all segments of the city, they provided a sense of hope after more than two years of squabbling, dissent, anger, and animosity. The plan led to the healing process, and for me, personally, that was a highly gratifying development.

Planning is the hidden face of a recovery, but there's also a public face, and voice. In a situation like that of post-Katrina New Orleans, local government needs to speak with one voice. By default, I became the voice for the recovery plan. Some people thought that was a good thing. Some people didn't, because I have a bad habit of saying what is on my mind. In any case, mayor Nagin had little patience with plans. I had to remind him that when I used the term "plan" I meant a prelude to action with a continuous set of projects that could be implemented.

MY FIRST TWO WEEKS IN CITY HALL WERE ILLUMINATING. Although I hadn't expected a big welcoming party, I was surprised at simply being put out to sea with almost no contact with anyone, including the mayor. I spent my first two weeks reviewing resumes, finding office space, and getting an office up and running with the help of the mayor's personnel assistant. But no one called to see what I was doing. No one seemed to want to know.

In January 2007, the city work force was less than half its pre-Katrina size of over 5,000. Mayor Nagin had been forced to cut the city payroll to meet the budget. Except for police and fire, the staff was significantly downsized. This downsizing was a blessing, Nagin told me, because he felt that a smaller, more technically proficient staff was more efficient to manage. But adding technology, he found, didn't generate the organizational efficiency he'd expected, because old staff traditions lingered.

The city was the first organization I'd worked in that had no written staff manual for employees or website of standard operating procedures. I asked for the city operating manuals so I could familiarize myself with systems in case they required modifications for the post-Katrina effort. I requested an early space in the new-employee induction program, so I could fathom how the city was run and who was responsible for the various units. When little resulted, I finally asked Becca O'Brien and others for these basic tools.

Word got back to the mayor about all that. And when I next saw him, he was upset with me for asking for such small things when we had a recovery to run. I knew this wasn't an issue to push.

However, I also knew that the absence of these fundamentals signaled a longer and deeper set of problems. So I set about developing my own orientation for myself. And when I found a dearth of public assets records that would indicate how much property the city owned and where it was, I realized that I had come to a city that was technologically advanced but administratively broken.

The mayor had spent his first term just getting the city computerized and replacing old-fashioned paper processes with digital records. I later discovered that he had been burned by his director of technology Greg Meffert, who used his post not only to modernize the city but also to create an empire for himself within the bureaucracy. It soon appeared, through 63 federal indictments, that Meffert had done well for more than the city. His alleged abuses made the mayor wary of aggressive senior staff, and strengthened his inclination to make loyalty the first test for those working for him.

Nagin did have a good, loyal executive cabinet of seven chief executive officers. We worked well for him in many ways. But the group members all felt they could be the supreme leader, much like the cabinet described in Doris Kearns Goodwin's *Team of Rivals: The Political Genius of Abraham Lincoln.* Some of those "rivals," like Salmon P. Chase, worked hard to show why they, not Lincoln, should have been president. In New Orleans, that attitude extended to me as well as the mayor: most of the time, I felt that several of Nagin's executive team thought, and tried to demonstrate, that they could run the recovery better than I could. As a result, teamwork was discussed but not practiced.

Nagin's cabinet had an inside team, or "cocoon," as my deputy Ezra Rapport called it. I wasn't part of this group of very close personal advisors. They met with the mayor informally and frequently, to steer him in directions they felt were in the best interests of the city. In the group were chief administrative officer (CAO) Brenda Hatfield, city attorney Penya Moses-Fields, right-hand deputy Kenya Smith, and head of communications Ceeon Quiett. It was an invisible, extra decision-making layer that could (and did) undercut or overturn cabinet decisions.

It became clear to me that I needed the cocoon's support for any major step I wanted to take. And I learned to seek its members' endorsements before taking matters to the mayor or making an important presentation to the cabinet.

Each Tuesday at 9 or 10 a.m., our executive team assembled in the mayor's large office around a dark mahogany table. The mayor took his customary seat, and the room came to order. An agenda with a large folio of attachments came with every meeting. The folio contained information on city services of vari-

Mayor

Chief Administrative Officer

- Homeland Security
- Finance
- Public Health
- Technology
- City Operations

Mayor's Executive Director of Recovery

- Infrastructure
- Resettlement
- Planning
- Economic Development
- Redevelopment

Communications Director

Intergovern-mental Affairs Director

City Attorney

City organization streamlined.

ous types, from fire responses to building permits to pending lawsuits against the city and press reports from around the nation. Each unit provided a short report of the highlights of the previous week. In some cases, the reports included data on specific items the mayor had requested to track crime, technology, and the recovery. The mayor's issues were first on the agenda. Although every executive staff member presented items for discussion, I presented the most. I did that because many issues that involved recovery transcended my own authority and required the support of other departments. In most cases, I included a memo and data or other materials to support my case.

I came to know each of the executive team, and succeeded in working with most of them collegially. I had learned from years as a manager that it's wise to collaborate with other managers you work with at the level that's comfortable for them. The mayor didn't give direct orders to anyone. You had to find your own way. He said more than once that he'd hired me because I wasn't from New Orleans and had worked with other mayors successfully.

He told he wanted me to work with the staff to do the recovery and not to run the recovery as another operation. So in this case it wasn't smart to try to get other senior staff to do things they could not or did not want to do. This rule applies in most management situations, and in disaster and recovery.

This was my view of the executive team and the other regularly invited guests as we assembled each week around the mayor's table:

Brenda Hatfield always sat to the mayor's immediate right. As CAO, she was by charter the second in command. Her staff and budget were the largest in the city. She was charged with all basic city services, from garbage pickup to police, fire, emergency, building, parks, and capital works.

Brenda, who has a Ph.D., is a smart and pert woman who was always immaculately and professionally dressed. She is quiet unless challenged. She presented few items, because most of her responsibilities were predictable and seldom involved other executive staffers.

Brenda welcomed me when I arrived. She provided good counsel and support throughout my tenure. She took the time to introduce me to important and useful people in the city. She was my best ally in the recovery.

We worked together well. Our primary interactions consisted of issuing requests for proposals from contractors. The issue that united us most was modernizing the city budgeting, management, and human resource systems. The mayor came into office with no modern management tools.

Hatfield used the crisis as a device for modernization. She embarked on a program to raise salaries of all staff at least to the median of Southern cities, and she put the city on a performance budget system. That required a clear, orderly organization with agency and unit goals and accountability measures. She forged the first links between budget and performance.

Brenda and I came to the conclusion that we had to outsource project management. Early in my tenure, we worked out an approach to bring in external contractors that she felt comfortable with. We supported one another's agendas. She and I wanted modern, efficient systems to run the city and as a bonus from the recovery.

Becca O'Brien, a Harvard Law School graduate, occupied the next chair and had the title counsel to the mayor. She is a tall, willowy woman with an athletic look who walks and talks fast. Becca told me she'd left a job in the White House a year after the storm, and had camped out in New Orleans for two months to get a job with the mayor. She not only got a job with him, she became one of his early confidants. Her office was only a few feet from his, a proximity that gave her considerable access. She acted as chief of staff, although no one had that official title.

I liked and trusted Becca. She gave me good feedback. She made sure that my views, even when opposed internally by some staff, got a good hearing from the mayor. She didn't take sides, and instead let my issues rise or fall on their merits. We might have disagreed on form but never content. She saw the value of using the UNOP results as support for our action plan. At the mayor's request, she did an audit of the recovery plan.

Becca seemed dedicated to empiricism. Her reports provided the mayor with added confidence that the Target Area Plan could and would work. She instituted an internal reporting and assessment process of the recovery to measure progress against our internal targets. (I could have argued, but didn't, to have the system located in my office.) We took advantage of her position to help advance and reinforce the recovery goals.

Kenya Smith was a wily young man of small stature with what my uncle Randy characterized as chutzpah. Kenya is talkative, and he speaks in spurts. His passions for the city are deep. Although his job on paper was to work with city council and state legislative representatives, he transformed it into a job of maintaining relations with all city organizations. He is well connected around the city.

In the middle of my first year, Kenya announced his plan to leave the office. I asked him to reconsider and pleaded with the mayor to intervene. He stayed for a few more months. During that period, he orchestrated our State Revolving Fund, which he was able to get from the State Bond Commission through a city-based bond issue backed by the city's future funds from FEMA and federal Community Block Grant funds. Finally, he got the legislation we needed to speed up the recovery process by getting through the Louisiana legislature a "design build" procedure that allows you to enter one contract for building rather than separate contracts for architects, builders, landscaping, and the like. Design build was opposed by the state contractors association on the grounds that it prevented small firms from successful bidding.

Kenya ran for William Jefferson's House of Representatives seat. Like many other aspirants, Kenya thought Jefferson would step down before a messy trial over his many federal counts for misuse of his post for financial gain. Kenya lost in the primary to Jefferson, only to see him soundly defeated by a Republican newcomer and later convicted in federal court for bribery.

Cynthia Sylvain-Lear was the saint of the recovery. A middle-aged woman with a quick wit and a great smile, she carried the recovery on her back—or, more precisely, in her voluminous notebooks. As Brenda's deputy, she came to most meetings and sat next to Kenya. She took on any role needed as we mobilized to move the recovery forward. She was the city's public memory.

Cynthia fought FEMA every step of the way until my staff and I took over much of that task. After opposing outsourcing, she championed it. She coordinated the myriad internal processes of the city so that we could move projects through the state, federal, and local bureaucratic systems as smoothly as possible. Because she understood how the city bureaucracy functions, she was able to facilitate difficult issues, ranging from finances to building priorities. I learned to respect Cynthia's institutional knowledge, and together we set priorities and timelines for rebuilding city facilities.

Penya Moses-Fields is an impressive person, an ex-athlete who still moves with an athlete's gait. As city attorney she was the city's conscience. Penya doled out legal advice with precision. Well prepared in all circumstances, she put me in my place on more than one occasion. She did that to make sure we were all playing by the right rules.

At meetings where we dealt with requests for proposals, Penya made sure the law and policy we were applying met the charter and state legal requirements and protocols. She was an aggressive lawyer, but had a delicate position as both city attorney and counselor to the mayor. She handled that position well, defeating a challenge from the city council over her serving as a mayoral advisor and tried to bring in outside attorneys. Clearly, Penya was a competitor.

We worked together best against common foes. For her part, Penya truly enjoyed vanquishing the opponents. She took on the former owners of a failed shopping center in New Orleans East. Before Katrina, the city had lent the developers money to build the center. It didn't perform well, and almost went bankrupt before the storm. The owners wanted to continue operating with additional city cash. We said no, and prevailed—here and in many other situations—through hard bargaining.

Penya enjoyed playing the bad cop role. More than once she provided legal and policy advice that allowed us to get things done by nimbly maneuvering through state rules. She didn't think we needed to outsource the recovery *or* use design build. But once the mayor approved both, she started staffing to meet the needs. We differed on using computerized contracting to expedite the processing of construction contracts. When I began my tenure in New Orleans, it took an average of three months to move a simple contract through all the city agencies for signature before the contract reached the mayor's desk. I thought this could and should be put into routine computerized systems that could cut the time to one day.

William M. (Bill) Chrisman was a late 2008 addition to the team as capital projects manager. Bill is a gruff, my way or no way guy. His knowledge of buildings was terrific but he was woefully ill equipped to work in a political bureaucracy that was hostile to new ideas, accountability, and direction. His instinct in meetings was to try to force his way rather than to coax others to his views. He didn't see the value in having the Project Development Unit coordinate projects across the bureaucracy or in using MWH, our outside project management contractor. As a result, he was marginalized early, which slowed the rebuilding process.

Julie Harris, a Sixties person, was a short, energetic, fast-talking, hardworking deputy to Kenya Smith when I first worked with her, and she later took on his job when he resigned. She also had a wider role of managing federal grants and relations. Julie is a nonstop activist. I got ten or more emails from her in a day when she got involved in a project. She's dedicated to the city and its government. I spent considerable time in her office gaining insights into the city and its people.

Ceeon Quiett is a small, pert lady with a soft voice. She was the mayor's communications chief, but had decided that her role extended to all city communications. I felt, and still feel, that as important as the mayor's image is, city agencies and departments also need to communicate, to present themselves as civic institutions and authoritative civil servants. People understandably want to talk to the boss. Because Ceeon presented Nagin as the only person who knew what was going on, he became the only source they trusted, and they had less confidence in what other agency heads had to say. I felt the need for more direct media outreach from my office. We never saw eye to eye on whether the Katrina recovery needed its own communications effort as a city function, and our relations were never what either of us had hoped for.

Ceeon did support the major recovery projects coming from my division—when she could get the mayor in them for a picture or press opportunity. We worked well together during and after Hurricane Gustav in 2008, and putting together the recovery websites and community forums.

We worked best on specific programs and projects, so I tried to get programs into her agenda to advance our mutual recovery goals. Once something got into Ceeon's program book, she executed it zealously.

Reginald (Reggie) Zeno, director of finance, is a soft-spoken, well-groomed man who looks like a banker. On our trip to New York to secure funding for recovery, he gained the confidence of the financial community, which would prove crucial to getting funds. He and I liked basketball and attended games together. We became partners in financial innovation, often combining our talents to find new ways to fund recovery operations.

If I ran a city, I would want Reggie as my finance chief and most of his team on my side. He's a light talker but a deep thinker, a role player with considerable skills that a boss needs to know when and how to employ. We found we could use one another in many situations.

Ezra Rapport, chief operating officer, a close friend from my Oakland years, came to New Orleans and became my close confidant in the recovery. He devised the recovery office organization, led our outsourcing efforts, and crafted the program to get projects from our city plan though state and federal approval processes. He is a hard charger with a blunt style, and although the mayor liked him, some people found him abrasive. He's also smart, overpowering most people with his brilliance.

I found that Ezra was especially valuable on tough issues where kid gloves didn't work. I liked to use him where the goals were clear, but the means to reach the goals might be fraught with thorny intergovernmental problems, especially between city and state. He left the city's employment with a long list of accomplishments, from revising the blight codes to getting NORA on the right track. He attracted many friends in the city bureaucracy, but also developed a long list of people who were glad to see him go.

Finally, the mayor. I felt like Mayor Nagin was a prince who conducted meetings much as did President Lincoln. He convened and led discussions, and waited for wisdom to emerge from the room. He didn't push his own ideas. He listened and drew people out. He would warn speakers of the ramifications of various courses of action. He would say things like, "Well, the Council will love that one. They'll have all my authority with that move." Or, "New Orleans East is the toughest place in the world to work. Are you sure of the players?"

Nagin was quick to praise and slow to scold. He liked ideas. He understood the need to get key people to act in a uniform direction. In his view, if he hired you, you should know your job and how to lead your people. He was not a walk-around manager; he brought everyone to his office. He also called large team meetings to push citywide changes in the bureaucracy and urged division heads to find ways to do the job. He didn't tell them how to do it. In my own case, he gave me explicit authority but never precise direction.

Nagin was generous, and he found ways to do nice things for people. In late December 2007, for example, I lay flat on my back in Ochsner Hospital. I was scheduled to go to a Louisiana Recovery Authority meeting in Baton Rouge to get final clearance for the city recovery funds. I was in no shape to travel by conventional means, so I asked Duce to organize an ambulance to take me to Baton Rouge. The mayor heard about my plans. He called me in the hospital to say, "I'm going, Doc. You stay in bed." He changed his entire schedule and went to Baton Rouge in my place.

Nagin took chances on people he trusted. He committed himself to the right things over intense criticism from within his own cocoon. Nagin is a spiritual person, at home with the scriptures. He's one of the best bosses I ever had, and my list of bosses is long. He gets the best from the team like a professional coach. And like a general manager, he brought in good players and let me as captain meld my team into a productive unit. The mayor and I spent a lot of time together, testifying 31 times to congressional and federal organizations as well as visiting foundations and other cities in the United States such as Philadelphia, as well as Panama and China, to gain knowledge of the kind of projects we might do in New Orleans

As recovery czar, my strategy with the mayor's cocoon was to get one or two of them on my side. If I needed only one, it was Penya, because she had the inside track to the top man. Unfortunately, this particular group of players, led by the mayor, needed a better system with which to manage a massive recovery that was overwhelming the existing bureaucracy. They were trying to navigate a complex, multifaceted, twenty-first-century recovery effort clinging to a byzantine, outdated, and lumbering administrative process.

THE MAYOR STARTED HIS SECOND TERM WITH ROUGHLY twenty senior staff, including those I've just described as his "cocoon," reporting directly to him. When I arrived, there were three direct line officers: myself, as director of recovery management, with a small team of 20; Brenda Hatfield, CAO, with several thousand employees; and Donna Addkison, chief development officer and head of economic development and housing, with about 200.

As I've indicated, Addkison and I couldn't get on the same page from the outset. We had only one meeting during my first six months, and that one at the mayor's insistence. He was apparently frustrated with her, too. After nearly a year, the entire executive team could see that Addkison's days were numbered, and the cocoon seemed to be plotting her demise. After one executive meeting in which the mayor hammered her, I ran into Brenda, his right-hand woman, and Penya, the city attorney, getting on the elevator. They knew Donna was on her way out.

After I arrived in New Orleans, I was ready to interview staff for my new Office of Recovery Management, the title the mayor had put before the city council for approval and funding. The organization chart included a deputy and key staff for four functions:

- Resources—to find additional funding from nongovernmental sources for the recovery and coordinate all forms of outside help and resources, including volunteers;

- Planning—to develop and monitor the recovery plan;
- Infrastructure and environment—to deal with the massive problems of prioritizing water and power restoration, and developing basic infrastructure resilience against future disasters;
- Settlement—to assist in housing, resettlement, and community development issues.

Among the first things I had to do as recovery czar was to try to begin retooling government, to pare down the number of different municipal operating boards and committees in the city, each with its own authority. We faced an unusual and difficult situation: there was no central governmental apparatus to direct the recovery. That was, and remains, New Orleans, and it was to make my job a lot harder, because the mayor, for whom I was working, did not control all the central institutions of government across the city/parish.

New Orleans is an inordinately complicated bureaucracy. Every new job has to go to the Civil Service Commission for approval. The commissioners wanted all the jobs to be paid at the salary of current city staff, even though these salaries were too low to attract competent staff. In fact, some positions, like architects, were vacant for years. Not only did they protect outdated salaries, they also had a bizarre practice of setting a single salary based on the last salary paid to the occupant of the post. So, if the last person's salary was high when you took the job, you got a good start. But if you wanted to transfer from another job into a new office, you might be told that the salary for the job was lower than the salary you were leaving, and that it couldn't be changed. I spent far too much time negotiating this system, and that's one of the reasons I wanted to contract out many of the better jobs for the recovery.

The Office of Recovery and Development—my group—had twenty staff, only five of them on the city payroll. I organized my own staff with the youngest qualified people I could find on the city payroll. In case there were any layoffs, I didn't want the young people to suffer. The rest of the staff drew grant salaries from a nonprofit we had to set up to bypass the byzantine city rules that couldn't accommodate new employees unless they were taken from the layoff list, and paid salaries insufficient for the qualified people we needed to attract. As it happened, staff who weren't on the city payroll worked for almost two months with no salaries, until the foundation grants arrived, and we put them on foundation funding that would only last two years. If the city didn't pick up these people's salaries after that, their jobs would disappear.

Among other staff, I brought aboard Jessie Smallwood, a colleague from my antipoverty days in California. She was close to people at the Ford Foundation. She worked with me to develop our grant proposal to help fund recovery planning and staffing. I had good connections at Ford, too. In the first funding, the Bill and Melinda Gates Foundation joined Ford to provide for an expanded staff for two years.

For example, we needed a deputy director for day-to-day recovery operations. We also required help—a resource position for raising more foundation and government money. We needed a person to coordinate our neighborhood projects; a person with environmental credentials for all the environmental issues associated with the recovery; and a staff person to examine local, state, and national policies that we might be able to use to get more recovery funds for New Orleans.

Staffing decisions and hiring were only the start of building an organization to support the recovery. Although we started putting together a team immediately, it would take two years to get our organization team and structure to the point required to do the job we needed to do.

■ ■ ■

Initially, my ORM staff and I had only planning responsibilities, with implementation authority required through the mayor. My staff was to develop project ideas from the UNOP and other plans. We came up with basic priorities for target areas, in consultation with neighborhood organizations, and then estimated funding needs for each project. Our budget guesses were not too far off. I had enough experience in building things to have a fairly good idea of costs and I had run more than one economic development nonprofit, so I had some idea of what social program costs were. Then we turned over the construction to Brenda's Capital Projects operation. This process was developed, under the mayor's direct control, for every part of the city.

I knew that recovery was a temporary process for any city, but I recognized the need to use the process as a catalyst to transform the New Orleans bureaucracy into a new and better institution, by employing many processes used *in* the recovery. One of the goals of recovery is to create new ways of working that break down the usual administrative "silos," by which each part of a government bureaucracy runs on its own internal rules. In a recovery, however, there are few rules. So while the emergency response is underway, it's important to use the opportunity to show how government can operate better.

I asked the mayor to give my post the designation deputy mayor. I based this request on previous experience in the two Oakland events, combined with observations in Los Angeles, New York, and Kobe. Coordination alone is not enough. Directing a recovery requires line authority with the ability to identify resources and commit them to the established priorities.

In September 2007, we were finally able to fashion a better administrative approach to New Orleans recovery. Donna Addkison had decided to leave, and my first impulse was to find a more cooperative colleague. In Ezra Rapport, I already had one. Ezra and I knew that a collaborative bureaucracy took several years to develop momentum, even under less pressure than we now faced in New Orleans. From my experience and from many conversations with disaster management colleagues worldwide, after Katrina and again after my appointment, I knew that there were essentially two options to transform this particular bureaucracy.

One approach was to build a separate empire within the existing city government, giving people power to take the initiative where needed. You patch up any holes and smooth out ruffled feathers, but you create a parallel government that operates above and around the bureaucracies to get the recovery done.

The other strategy is to hire a strong individual leader who will push department heads and restructure the government in a modern, professional way. You lead so adroitly that people feel they're dealing with power, and they do what you need them to do.

What *doesn't* work is to appoint somebody like me, give the person few resources, and then rely on him to play the bad guy who beats up on peers to get things done when he has no true authority over them. In 2007, to get things done with my small staff, we started out trying to harass and harangue people who knew the place better than I did. As one said, mimicking black street argot, "We be here when you be gone."

After a few meetings, Mayor Nagin decided over lunch with me on a hybrid approach that merged my Office of Recovery Management and Addkison's former Office of Housing and Economic Development into one operation, the Office of Recovery and Development Administration (ORDA). I liked this solution, presented to the city council on November 27, 2007, and it was a major milestone in the recovery, because with this organization I could control a range of essential activities associated with the recovery, from planning and dispensing permits to blight reduction and economic development. We were transformed from a group that simply made plans to the arm that identified projects to rebuild and design, and made sure that the projects were in the correct target areas. If messy, the new organization was nonetheless essential. We used it to craft a system for using the Target Area Plan as a template for community-rebuilding processes that ranged from commercial districts to housing.

The ORDA team grew from my original group of twenty to a staff organization of more than 200 that took on three primary tasks to support *long-term* recovery:

1. Retool the government for the recovery, as part of taking the next step from creating projects to altering the bureaucracies that manage them. For example, the post-Katrina capital works program for recreation facilities had to build safety and sustainability into new or repaired buildings, and align rebuilding with a new cluster concept for putting as many city buildings as possible close to or in target areas' commercial strips.

2. Secure funds. In a recovery, that's not a one-shot job. Priorities change, so you need different sources of money, and, especially, creative blends of public and private funding. We embarked on several state programs like Gulf Opportunity bonds (GO Zone), which amounted to federal underwriting for development projects that assisted directly in the physical and economic recovery of devastated counties. This was debt financing that the local governments could endorse but not pursue on their own. My staff, when they became aware of the significance of these bonds, tried to steer projects into target areas by using the city endorsement as leverage.

   We also tapped into new funding sources from the federal Departments of Transportation and Agriculture, as well as HUD, to create programs that would augment public, private, and nonprofit projects. Among other examples we bridged economic development programs to bring grocery stores into neighborhoods that hadn't had a store that sold fresh produce for decades.

3. Develop programs and projects for implementation. This meant working inside the city to use our Disaster Community Development Block Grants (DCDBG) resources for various city renewal projects. We were temporarily hamstrung by the complexities of the DCDBG grant administration process, which featured a nine-foot wall chart checklist of instructions and rules that had to be satisfied in devising

our economic development programs so that we could use city, state, federal, and private sector funds together.

We combined disaster funds with other city monies to craft new ways to meet community needs such as the restoration of a historic black golf course, and we leveraged new private resources to rebuild libraries as community social and cultural venues.

The linchpin of New Orleans restoration, however, was the project of rebuilding the housing stock. With NORA, we developed creative homeownership programs to raise the ownership percentage in all neighborhoods. NORA finally yielded to our demands because it wanted to be a significant part of the recovery and this was the only route. NORA tried to get funds from foundations and state and federal government. But the requests were turned down because NORA couldn't say this was what the mayor and council wanted. No one wanted to fund competing recovery organizations. The mayor authorized our team to explore options to reach our defined goal of $300 million in mortgage assistance for homeownership. We reached this goal with the nation's largest assistance program, which we designated primarily for the target areas.

Another program, championed by council member Willard-Lewis, was called the Lot Next Door. It allowed owners to acquire vacated properties next to their own. Willard-Lewis and I got the program going, with the reluctant help of NORA. I asked her to insert a provision to prevent speculators from using owners as pawns to get property cheap and resell it.

It isn't possible to achieve neighborhood improvements in New Orleans without blight reduction. We embarked on the first large-scale comprehensive programs in New Orleans history to reduce blight by combining several offices with varying legal authorities into a single one. For example, we merged the adjudication courts for sanitation and environmental blight into one court. We also introduced neighborhood sweeps that brought police and other enforcement units to bear on dilapidated properties.

Community economic development was as important as large-scale initiatives. Our approach included the establishment of more than a dozen new neighborhood commercial-revitalization programs to make distressed communities more commercially vital than they were before Katrina.

We broadened that focus to include the design of a new public-private partnership championed by council member Arnie Fielkow. It resembled the vehicles we used when I led Oakland Sharing the Vision, and when I served

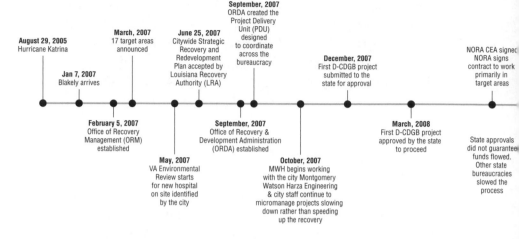

August 29, 2005
Hurricane Katrina

Jan 7, 2007
Blakely arrives

March, 2007
17 target areas
announced

February 5, 2007
Office of Recovery
Management (ORM)
established

June 25, 2007
Citywide Strategic
Recovery and
Redevelopment
Plan accepted by
Louisiana Recovery
Authority (LRA)

May, 2007
VA Environmental
Review starts
for new hospital
on site identified
by the city

September, 2007
ORDA created the
Project Delivery
Unit (PDU)
designed
to coordinate
across the
bureaucracy

September, 2007
Office of Recovery &
Development Administration
(ORDA) established

December, 2007
First D-CDGB project
submitted to the
state for approval

October, 2007
MWH begins working
with the city Montgomery
Watson Harza Engineering
& city staff continue to
micromanage projects slowing
down rather than speeding
up the recovery

NORA CEA signed
NORA signs
contract to work
primarily in
target areas

March, 2008
First D-CDGB project
approved by the state
to proceed

State approvals
did not guarantee
funds flowed.
Other state
bureaucracies
slowed the
process

Recovery timeline.

on the housing board in Oakland and on the New York Partnership. The idea in these cases was to devise a public-private economic development corporation to take the lead in attracting and keeping businesses in the city. New Orleans needed the financial support of local business leaders and the active involvement of minority firms and community groups. When I finally left the city in 2009 the program was stillborn: the mayor had withdrawn support because he sensed big businesses were involving themselves only to get public funds for their own purposes, and had little inclination to work with low-income neighborhoods.

▪ ▪ ▪

Administratively, the post-storm recovery was entangled in complicated lines of authority and management. The Parish and City of New Orleans occupy the same space, but are different legal entities whose agencies operate independently or semi-independently. We had to deal with too many of those agencies—more than 60, each with an operating board and committee in the city and a separate jurisdiction. The mayor can appoint members to these boards, but the city charter makes them independent. The Sewerage and Water Board, for example, sets its own policies and direction through a commission, and the City Park Commission, which is independent of the city government, even collects and uses its own taxes without city oversight.

The administrative problem for the recovery came down to this: all these entities were submitting independent requests to FEMA. They acted like independent jurisdictions. That put me in an unusual situation, bereft of any central governmental apparatus that the mayor (my boss) controlled.

My take on the situation is that as New Orleans leadership changed from white to black, the need to isolate parts of the city from the central management became paramount for upper class whites and some middle-class blacks. City entities important to white communities were insulated from black rule by separating them from city governance.

But for recovery to work, we'd need to coordinate the building programs so that we didn't waste money putting up a building, only to have to tear up the street to provide the underground utilities for it. And we needed to do all of this in some smooth, sequential, and logical way.

Such a variety of agencies does have advantages. It brings innovation and considerable quality management, and most of the time there was close coordination and cooperation among the parish and city entities. Nonetheless, as my favorite management professor used to say, "Coordination is costly." He was certainly correct as regards my experiences in the administration of the Katrina recovery.

Attempting to move information among city/parish organizations inside city government consumed a lot of my time as executive director of ORDA. Since these organizations didn't report to me or to the mayor, I could control them only if they had to pass through my office for federal funds.

In other words, I would have to use control over outside resources to corral unwieldy and uncontrolled fiefdoms.

In September 2007 I finally got authority from FEMA headquarters in Washington to act as a pass-through for federal funds, along with an executive order from the mayor to do so. With this authority in hand, we formed a parish-wide council of organizations. It became the chief body for the recovery, and met quarterly to assess resources and directions. Thanks to a high degree of voluntary collaboration, the council's efforts worked better than the federal coordinator's interventions.

The parish-wide council first met in early April 2008 to set priorities. I recognized right away that encouraging conversation among all the agencies was more important than exercising power over them. So I hosted meetings with several of them on a variety of topics, such as education and job training, to let Washington know we were collectively on the same page. The local transportation agency and school district, for example, coordinated their efforts to use the same central messages in their requests to Washington and Baton Rouge.

I also set monthly meetings with the FEMA regional team to review how the parish was faring with all agencies and other entities. This approach worked. I initially expected that the parish-wide group would generate considerable clout over major matters like the direction of economic development. That occurred to a degree, though not according to my expectations. The council declined to take formal stands on any issues. But its member organizations adopted support strategies that helped us move forward on major projects. On a wide variety of topics, from environmental hazard reduction to coordinating high school special-emphasis curricula, my staff directors were able to form council working groups that matched the economic directions of the Nagin administration. Thus the parish-wide council became the single entity for coordinating multiple governmental agency projects like large-scale infrastructure.

■ ■ ■

The next task in creating an administrative system that could advance the recovery was to streamline the internal disaster projects. These were projects that could be financed by specially authorized federal disaster community development funds from the regular, unexpended block grant and city bond funds. We needed to organize and prioritize these projects. And each fund type had different eligibility requirements and rules for how it could be expended.

The city had limited resources to construct and repair buildings, so in April 2007 I asked Brenda Hatfield if I could put out requests for proposals (RFPs) to bring in architects and a project management firm to manage the several hundred building projects we would have to get underway in the next few months. Administratively, I wanted to outsource this part of the recovery.

Brenda was enthusiastic. The city had only four staff architects, and their salaries were too low to attract the kinds of fulltime professionals we needed for this complex work. We conducted interviews and selected 17 architectural firms to start developing scopes of work for the buildings eligible for FEMA funds. We also interviewed project management firms, and ultimately selected Montgomery Watson Harza (MWH).

It was tasked to coordinate the several hundred projects. Based in Denver, its work ranged from supervising the architects' project "scoping" to putting the projects out to bid to making sure they were cost effective and on schedule. Everything from soup to nuts landed in MWH's lap.

The selection of MWH was a matter of expediency. We didn't have in-house the human resources required to design, organize, and contract to reconstruct city buildings and related infrastructure. As I've said, city staff had been downsized to a few key positions. Capital projects had only four or five people, none with the depth of experience required to manage so many projects and put them out to bid or monitor construction.

Also, based on my experience in Oakland, Ezra Rapport and I concluded that we had to have a professional team with the experience to manage a construction project equivalent in size to rebuilding San Francisco after the 1906 earthquake—and to deal with all the FEMA complexities. Dealing with FEMA was time-consuming and heartbreaking. In other recoveries I've worked on, either the state or FEMA advanced the funds so that vital facilities could be brought up and running. For the first two years of my "czarship," we would receive little from FEMA with which to repair the city's police and fire stations. The agency wound up giving us a comparative pittance—roughly 15 percent of what we required. The city had to take $30 million from its tight budget to repair vital facilities quickly, with no assurance that this huge amount would ever be reimbursed. FEMA was a slow, bumbling operation that demanded an enormous amount of paperwork. We often discovered that our requests to the agency had been lost or had been changed with no warning.

The city's slow and bureaucratically hobbled hiring process would take too long for us to hire much-needed staff. Moreover, the need for skills to do engineering and project management required very expensive short-term personnel who wouldn't be needed after the first phase of the recovery. It wasn't clear how we could hire and then terminate these people in the existing bureaucracy. Finally, FEMA pays overhead for contractors, but only a limited amount for internal staff. So, it made good sense for all these reasons to use a large firm that had all the specialists we needed for basic project design and to monitor the progress of construction.

Once we developed and implemented a contract with the help of several outside advisors, including the head of the Superdome, who brought a lot of good sense to all this, and after substantial internal debate, we created an internal organization, the Project Development Unit (PDU), to coordinate and set priorities to guide MWH and coordinate all New Orleans bureaucracies and agencies to deliver federal or state funds to projects. In many cases, we had to decide which funding source was best for a particular project, because it is against the law to commingle federal funds. We met every Wednesday to check on such important elements as gas and electrical hook-ups and interior furnishings. Project "siting," or in some cases rebuilding at a new site, was also part of the job. So, too, were coordinating all incoming funds and determining how they might be leveraged with available sources.

Project level approvals were made by the PDU, with the mayor giving the final okay. The big problems remained, however. The city staff refused to recognize the work of MWH and redid it for no good reason, slowing the effort almost to a standstill.

After a nationwide search, we hired Bill Chrisman as director of capital projects to supervise and direct the physical rebuilding process. Chrisman became a source of contention. He wanted to run the rebuilding process himself and use MWH as needed. My experience with Ezra Rapport convinced us that a managed external contractor would turn out better than using day-to-day operations staff. Moreover, FEMA would pay for this approach, as part of project management expenses, whereas it would not pay to augment permanent staff.

In short, we tried to outsource project management of the recovery while retaining overall direction for recovery priorities and funding.

For capital projects, I wanted a staff that had its own lawyers and accounting systems but wouldn't have to get involved in routine things that could be outsourced. Here I had only limited success, because city staff and Chrisman weren't familiar with supervising outside project managers. So, we started down the same path, with Chrisman redoing MWH work rather than simply ensuring the outcomes, which delayed the recovery administratively.

■ ■ ■

With the parish-wide council, management outsourcing of building projects, and streamlining of city bureaucracy, we had an administrative system in place to move the recovery forward. We were on a tight schedule, however, as we needed to commit all the disaster funds and start all the building projects on our priority list before the mayor left office in May 2010. This was hard to do since, aside from FEMA reimbursements, we received no direct federal funds until a year after the LRA approved the city's recovery budget. The city council kept pushing me to get started, even though, in my November 2008 annual report, I presented a chart showing how long it was taking for money to funnel from the feds to the state and finally to the city.

The schedule was tight for me personally, too. I was on leave from the University of Sydney and had been away from my family for over a year, I'd been struggling with health problems, and my remaining tenure in New Orleans was shorter than the recovery timetable.

But I recalled the passage in Doris Kearn Goodwin's 2005 *A Team of Rivals: The Political Genius of Abraham Lincoln*, which cites Secretary Seward's diary at the end of one of the great Civil War battles: "if my own anxiety is so great, what must his [the president's or, for me, the mayor's] solicitude be, after waiting three long weary years of doubt and disaster?"

THE NEW ORLEANS RECOVERY WAS LARGELY ABOUT THE politics of money and who controlled it: city or state, black or white, rich or poor, downtown or the neighborhoods. In the recovery, there was money on the table. It could be used to determine who came back to New Orleans, and who didn't. Much of the recovery played out at the contentious vector of money, land, housing, and race politics.

Four months after I took over the recovery, we received preliminary approval from the LRA for the $417 million in recovery block grant funds from the federal government. The state viewed that money as *state*, not New Orleans, funds. This was unusual. In my earlier experiences with such grants, they went directly to the city, once the city budget had been approved. Instead, in this case, the state preempted our grants by reviewing every project, thus increasing the time spent in processing and slowing down everything.

In the Kathleen Blanco administration, parts of the state bureaucracy, such as the audit department, were hostile in this review. The administration seemed to assume that New Orleans was going to steal the money and that city officials were only there to take the money, not to get anything worthwhile done. Our city council president was under indictment at the time, as were several members of the school board, and a recent member of city council was almost certainly going to be indicted for using zoning as a cash machine. To the state, the idea of local public officials having the opportunity to decide how the money was spent in New Orleans sounded either foolish or outrageous.

New Orleans was subject to ridiculous oversight for the use of federal funds. The city, like all American cities, spent millions of dollars every year of similar funds with no state involvement. Furthermore, the allocation to the state was viewed by the feds as a mere legal pass-through, not a state device to determine the city's recovery. No other state that had similar funds subjected localities to any standards like the ones Louisiana was imposing.

This struggle to gain leverage and control of the recovery funds, and hence the recovery itself, had started long before I arrived. I walked into it. The infamous green dots were used by the BNOB committee to designate areas, largely black lower- and middle-class neighborhoods, that were to be transformed into wetlands. Post-recovery plans put forward by several groups put strong emphasis on local economic recovery and especially small business and the arts. But the real contest was housing for whom? To reassure blacks who worried that post-storm New Orleans would become majority white after three decades of black demographic and political domination, Mayor Nagin used the term "chocolate city." His language, in turn, kindled fears in whites about a return to the city of low-income, public housing residents.

In 2002, the Department of Housing and Urban Development (HUD) had taken over management of New Orleans public housing because, as HUD stated, "even before Hurricane Katrina struck, many New Orleanians were ill-served by aging, poorly maintained public units." Damage from the 2005 storms, including mold, further weakened the structures, which led to the final decision not to reoccupy most of the city's public housing, and to tear down most of the units. That threatened not only a substantial part of the housing for blacks, but also black political power.

The political equation was easy to understand. Many of New Orleans's black people lived in public or subsidized low-income accommodations. These accommodations numbered more than 17,000, and they were extraordinarily segregated, with 95 percent occupancy by African Americans, the largest such concentration in the nation. Most black residents were renters. Furthermore, New Orleans had one of the lowest rates of homeownership in the nation, 45 percent, two-thirds of the U.S. average.

HUD's post-storm shuttering of all the largest public housing facilities in the city seriously impaired black political organization. So Nagin's remark about "chocolate city" had a major impact: it energized many New Orleans whites, who realized that, with no "public housing vote" for the first time in decades, they might actually have the numbers to install white political leadership.

The mayor got off to a shaky start after his reelection. It wasn't clear whose side he was on. The BNOB green dots threatened to turn many traditionally African American communities into park land, and the closure of public housing and the loss of small pockets of low-income homeowners in the Ninth Ward and similar low-lying areas suggested that black homeowners and renters would have few places to live in New Orleans. The black community started talking of a white conspiracy to retake political control. People love to imagine conspiracies, and that theory swept through the city and beyond: it was repeated in the national media.

The black public housing vote was important, as my activist friend MT and the mayor reveal in this exchange at the time of my appointment:

MT

Thanks for the advice. I have kept this on my top priority list and have been working to reach a win-win. Spoke with Cynthia W yesterday about this subject. I believe we have a good shot at reaching a compromise sooner than you may think. I will, however, discuss your recommendations with Dr. Blakely and advise.

Peace,

C. Ray Nagin - Mayor

Bringing New Orleans Back! — — — — — — — — — — — — —

Subject: BLAKELY APPOINTMENT, JEFFERSON'S REELECTION AND PUBLIC HOUSING DEMOLITION

GOOD MORNING MR. MAYOR:

Congratulations on the Blakely appointment. History will record this decision as a defining moment in your legacy. I pray that he will do you and we the citizens proud. We in civil society will do everything that we can to assist in the success of [Blakely's] department.

Congratulations for helping to derail the shadow train again. It was especially sweet given all the comparisons to your own reelection. The Jefferson victory was good for the city despite the naysayers. However, it now raises the question of the appropriateness of public housing demolition to a different level, given his opposition. Maxine Waters is also likely to oppose demolition as the only alternative. Given the level of growing local, federal and public opposition, now might be the time to reconsider whether demolition is the only option. There are other models of revitalization that don't result in massive displacement and gentrification, as the present approaches are likely to do. New Orleans has not even explored or discussed such options. That is precisely what makes the HANO [Housing Authority of New Orleans] decision suspect. It was made unilaterally without a critical examination of the variety of options available at a time that we desperately need affordable housing. Everyone including HANO might benefit from open and transparent discourse on this matter.

I humbly suggest and recommend that you request that Dr. Blakely review the basis of the HANO decision, consider the options and develop recommendations to you and the Council within 60 days. Then you, the residents, nonprofit and other interested stakeholders can explore successful alternative models that might uniquely serve New Orleans better than the one dimensional conclusions to demolish the 4 developments completely.

Please give consideration to a review, given the need to integrate all recovery plans into a wholistic framework. That would display another level of your leadership which your base would appreciate and greatly benefit from. Folks on the ground are quite intense in their organized opposition. While they are organizing direct action campaigns, they are also seeking a creative way out for everyone. Having the Recovery Department conduct a review to examine the state of the art and best practices in revitalizing public housing residents and their living environment is a win win for you, the residents, and the city. A review would also reduce any potential or likely opposition to your emerging Baton Rouge and Wash. DC recovery Agendas if the Agenda includes the proposed HANO demolitions. As we speak, there is evidence that some Congressional and citizen advocates are also reviewing HANO's decisions. You could be ahead of the curve on this one and gain additional status for the justice agenda

Peace,

The mayor didn't consult me very much about the demolition of public housing. But I offered him and his team two ideas. First, since the city had a shortage of affordable housing for laborers, make sure the tear-down is orderly enough to accommodate workers who might want to occupy the units prior to total destruction. Second, keep some of the best buildings for reuse as education or community space, because rebuilding this space entirely would be very expensive. Other than these ideas, and with the wheels already in motion, I kept my distance from the public housing question and concentrated instead on getting HANO to secure or tear down storm-damaged single-family and other small-unit facilities all over the city.

A prevalent ambition for middle-income groups, both black and white, was to rebuild the city by working with people not dependent on welfare. An African American resident of Pontchartrain Park, whose father headed the public housing agency, said to me at a community clean-up: "Those people shouldn't be allowed to come back. They hurt us all"—one of many striking illustrations of the city's "black-black" internal divisions. During my first few months in New Orleans, those sentiments were voiced many times by prominent blacks, who said openly and forthrightly that they didn't want any more public or subsidized housing built in the city, especially in middle-class New Orleans East.

The message was clear: everyone wanted the low-income public housing *votes*, but almost no one supported the notion of bringing back the tenants of public housing who possessed those votes, for fear that problems of poverty and crime would return with them.

Anxiety over the reappearance of low-income blacks was predictably high on the agenda of white civic leaders. Their deep feelings came home to me when a white businessmen's group asked me to lunch on St. Charles Avenue. I had barely sat down before my head table companions asked me about "crime groups, tax eaters, and property destroyers." After several more provocative remarks, I didn't eat much lunch. I just made a short talk, and left so soon after that Duce was surprised to see me. He asked me if the food was bad.

"Yes, very bad," I replied

In my first few weeks on the job, leaders of white civic groups showed me a plan for where and how they wanted recovery funds to be spent.

The "how" of the plan emerged in meetings with Donald Powell, President George W. Bush's Gulf Coast recovery coordinator. Powell postponed and rescheduled our first meeting several times, so I was never sure when or even if he would arrive. He didn't attend the press conference to announce the Target Area Plan. But in March 2007, a few days after that event, he came to my office purportedly to discuss post-Katrina progress and to present his views on how the recovery funding might be spent.

"What do you think of using nonprofit entities to carry out your Target Area Plan?" he asked me. My ears shot up. I pointed out that I had run nonprofits, and didn't consider them good vehicles for direct government-to-government business. He smiled, yet nonetheless suggested that such an organization could contribute to recovery funding, and then left into the night.

My profound concern here was that the nonprofit idea was a reversion to the past, when small groups, beyond public scrutiny, used public funds for a variety of purposes. New Orleanians would form an organization with a noble stated purpose and then use it for personal gain. Many nonprofits had misused state and federal funds, and indictments had followed.

I was also alarmed by the notion that I'd be reporting to a board that might direct me to use federal funds in ways inconsistent with the recovery plan, similar to what NORA was proposing. Under those circumstances I could end up the scapegoat for their actions, or responsible for spending federal funds in wrongly prioritized ways, even if they were legal. I really didn't want to associate myself with an organization run by a board that had authority over me and could fire me if I didn't follow their directives.

My short association with Joe Williams, NORA's new executive director, made it clear to me that things would head in that troubling direction, no matter who led NORA or any similar nonprofits. Nonprofits have a habit, I surmised from what I heard from local civic leaders and my staff, of becoming money shelters in New Orleans, and too many of the people who run them end up indicted. I would be even more reluctant if an ex-mayoral candidate, whose name came up prominently in this scheme, became the de facto unelected recovery mayor, as several insiders in the mayor's team described this person as trying to become mayor through this nonprofit back door.

Several conversations I had with New Orleans-based federal law enforcement people heightened my suspicion and anxiety. They let me know that they were going to "nail anyone" who put their fingers in the cookie jar. A few months later the city hired an independent investigator, who vowed openly that he was going to "get me" for misspending public funds. He thought that I was going to try to shield *myself* from public scrutiny by hiding behind a nonprofit.

Over the next few weeks, Powell became more explicit with his plan to put the money into some form of trust that would distribute it and keep it from what he called "political tinkering."

To be even-handed, the recovery ideas he advanced weren't outlandish. He, and others, wanted investment in areas that they thought would jump-start the economy and reduce the city's low-income, dependent population. Whereas the Target Area Plan would catalyze investments all over town, and focus on rebuilding neighborhoods, Powell was focusing on ways to bring cash into the city with larger showpiece developments that would, by his reasoning, jump-start the economy, too. That approach was not explicitly aimed, to be fair, at race or class imbalance, even if it subtly had that effect; it was aimed at remaking the city into a smaller unit in line with a less dependent, smaller population, down from over 600,000 to what appeared to be a new base of just under 400,000.

The core of the new plan, somewhat similar to BNOB's approach, was to revitalize a section of downtown, near the Superdome, which had been so badly damaged that it looked like a war zone. This approach paid scant attention to poor neighborhoods. The reasoning was that middle-class areas above the flood line would come back with only a little help, while less viable poor areas would fail, and should be allowed to fail and wither, thereby shrinking the city's footprint. Versions of this idea resurfaced continuously in the *Times-Picayune*.

On several occasions, I mentioned my conversations with Powell to Mayor Nagin. The mayor was nonplussed. "You hear lots of things around here, man," he said.

I thought the mayor's dismissal of the idea was the end of the Powell et al. initiative. But then matters intensified and became more contentious. I'd asked the NORA board to give me a plan for using its resources to buy properties and fix up commercial and residential land, with the target areas as top priority. My approach, I thought, would provide a basis for a contract between the city and NORA for the release of funds, because I had no other vehicle with which to revitalize commercial and residential areas of the city, especially the poorest areas.

NORA's board, however, wanted to pick the low-hanging fruit and do business deals with developers in middle-income or gentrifying areas, to create a self-supporting financial structure for the organization that would survive well past the recovery. Low-income property might be a loser for them, and not generate profits for future operations. NORA didn't hide this ambition, and many of the most influential insiders in the business community supported the cause to build a governmental entity outside City Hall's control that could remove blight and rekindle areas for private sector investments. They had in mind areas such as the distressed warehouses and abandoned buildings along the Mississippi waterfront that contamination and structural damage had made too risky for development, even before Katrina. Now, these areas could be a gold mine for local entrepreneur-developers if the risks were reduced for building.

Although operating in the target areas seemed sensible to me, the NORA board balked. Its members declared that they'd put together their own recovery plan and asked the mayor to provide them with the funds to do it. The ensuing argument escalated into public name calling and red meat for the press.

The mayor and I, with the help of a cogent memo by Becca O'Brien in defense of our position, held our ground. I told NORA that the city had every right to dictate how its money should be spent. Moreover, I noted, the approved Citywide Recovery (Target Area) Plan provided the mandate for all public spending—federal, state, and city. As the situation grew tenser, I declined invitations to go to NORA board meetings and sent my deputy, Jessie Smallwood, in my place.

Finally, after weeks of acrimony, in late spring 2007 I met with NORA and the LRA to work out how the state would transfer the hundreds and perhaps thousands of homes it bought from flood victims back to the city for reuse. The LRA was concerned that if owners sold those houses to the state, as they could do, the city would have to deal with thousands of abandoned and deteriorating dwellings. That blighted housing would retard the recovery, since no one would want to live next to such a building.

The LRA had the duty to solve this problem with state money and state eminent domain authority to seize abandoned properties. We agreed in a productive meeting that the state would form a trust fund to buy the housing, with NORA acting as the agent to put the properties back on the market or raze them to create new, buildable parcels.

This was a complicated scheme, because the total number and locations of the abandoned dwellings wouldn't be known until Road Home, the state agency responsible for purchasing the homes or lending funds to rehabilitate them, finished its work. Road Home was an enormously cumbersome operation, intended to provide homeowner relief of up to $150,000 based on the pre-storm value of the property and the extent of its damage. The process became so bogged down with legal bureaucracy that many people with necessary proof of ownership but modest resources simply gave up and never returned home. Even most of those who received the full settlement couldn't rebuild a place of comparable size on Road Home funds alone.

Road Home was a quagmire, and I tried to keep my organization from any direct involvement with it, for fear of sapping our energy. Nonetheless, we received each day at least a handful of complaints from irate citizens who believed that, as director of recovery, I had sole authority over all federal and state funds.

The entire program to decide where we'd focus our vacant housing plan was further stymied by federal and state privacy laws that kept us in the dark about which homeowners had decided to sell their houses to the state. We all agreed, however, that NORA was the best agency to take over the vacant units from the state and condemn those whose owners failed to return. Vacant housing was NORA's pre-storm mandate.

As the housing meeting closed amicably, one of the LRA board members said to me, "Maybe NORA would be a better agency to administer *all* recovery funds."

On the surface, that made sense. Housing was a big issue. But as I pointed out to the board member, the recovery was much bigger than abandoned housing. We also had streets and public buildings to repair; and the city had to kick-start the recovery of large and small businesses alike. Furthermore, my Recovery Management Office was subject to direct public control, and to accountability and oversight by the city council, in a way that NORA wasn't.

Even before this meeting, I was already aware through my various sources, including MT, that some sort of subterfuge was in the air.

Indeed, Powell came back to me a week later and renewed his suggestion that a nonprofit board be formed in a way that would meet my needs to administer the recovery funds. Powell's persistence raised yet more alarms. Powell was the president's representative. And he was supposed to be our advocate, so why was he suggesting ways to remove federal funds from public oversight? This idea didn't meet the smell test for me.

I went to the mayor again, and found him aware of Powell's insistence that we establish another body to carry the funds. Becca O'Brien, the mayor told me, had a draft memorandum of understanding written by one of the former mayoral candidate which proposed, as I understood the idea, to transfer the federal recovery funds to a new nonprofit corporation under the direction of NORA or another agency.

I was furious. "If that's the decision," I said, "I quit."

The mayor relented. "Doc," he told me, "It is your show. You run the recovery the way you want to. You do what is best."

I smiled and replied, "Mayor, I'm an old quarterback. I'll call my own plays."

The battle went on. Over the next several months, from May to November 2007, NORA board members, out of control, made wild accusations in the press about Mayor Nagin and me withholding funds so they couldn't do the recovery job.

As pressure escalated, the NORA board chairman had the good sense to propose a private, off-the-record meeting to cool things down. It was held in my office as a telephone conference: their board and staff members on one side; Becca and me on the other.

Afterward, one of the NORA representatives told me confidentially, "*You should be the head of NORA, with Joe [Williams, then its CEO] given some form of operational deputy job. That way, all the recovery funds would be in one place. Besides, you should have been the head of NORA in the first place.*"

I looked at him and responded disingenuously that I'd think about it. Moving federal funds around was just what my personal attorney in Oakland, Peter Turner, had warned me about. I called Peter. He thought that if I made the wrong move, I might end up accused of conspiracy to divert federal funds without proper city council or governmental oversight.

I realized that I'd better document all this.

The NORA plot thickened. In late February, just a week or so before I was to present the city's consolidated recovery plan to the LRA, two Rockefeller Foundation representatives and an LRA staffer called to arrange a weekend lunch with a highly regarded board chairman, David Voelker. I agreed to the meeting, but took a staff person and Duce with me. Later I put these notes in the file:

11:32 A.M.

At Martin Wine Cellar in Metairie

Meeting with Mr. Voelker was at the instigation of Rockefeller Foundation....I had met him on one other occasion and had seen him as a member of the Louisiana Recovery Authority.

This meeting was apparently organized to set a new direction for the recovery.

As we ordered meals, I explained that I could not accept any food or other freebies from anyone and could not meet with anyone alone—to protect myself from accusations of special deals or even bribes. Thus, my assistant was attending with me and listening to the entire meeting discussion. She would not, however, be participating.

Voelker opened the discussion by noting that he had become a close personal advisor to the governor through means he could not quite understand. He was, he said, also close to the president of the United States and to Chairman Powell. As he characterized it, Powell spends most of his time in the New Orleans region in Voelker's offices.

He laid out a scenario in which NORA would be a conduit for the $300–$600 million destined for the City of New Orleans. He stated that he and Chairman Powell had been conversing over the past several weeks on how to divert these funds to another entity and that NORA was ideal for this purpose. He said some other parties were involved and said Scott Cowen, the president of Tulane, might be one of them. He also suggested that others in the city were putting together various ways of ensuring that the federal funds flow to the place they felt was safe from interference—from the city council and others. He suggested this would be good for me since I would have a good board that could act as my shield (he used the word "protection") in the recovery process, because hard decisions were required.

At this point, I opined that a strong support structure *was* a good idea but that NORA was not a good vehicle for many reasons. I noted that the structure of the recovery committee formed by the city council was adequate. He replied that the council committee was *not* a good mechanism and that something smaller would work better. He said a meeting was going to be held in the White House, where this would be laid out to the president. In addition, the decisions made would flow back to the governor; he would be having dinner with her on Feb. 25, and all this was to be discussed then. He suggested that if NORA were the chosen instrument, a new board membership would be put in place and the current members save one or two others would remain. Joe Williams would be relegated to some lesser administrative post in this scenario. This was not discussed further beyond my saying Joe was a fine administrator, and this seemed unfair and unlikely.

Voelker felt he had the capacity to make any change in NORA, its board, and its mission that he wanted. He referred to Powell's intimate involvement in this arrangement.

I suggested the goal might be fine, but the means were flawed. First, the current makeup and goals of NORA were not appropriate to achieve the purposes he was outlining at this point. He countered with a reference to Virginia Boulet's drafting an MOU to bypass the city council and place the funds in a different set of accounts; I did not comment on that. He said the White House knew this and supported it.

The meeting ended amicably, with me expressing a wish to see a good mechanism established to do the job of recovery but grave reservations about the use of

NORA as a means to achieve such an end. Voelker suggested that a levee board might be used, but this involved complications which he didn't elaborate on. He was certain that the money was better in the hands of people who could steer it appropriately than in the hands of those who could not—and the latter obviously included the city council's recovery committee. He said that this nonprofit-board approach would only work if I concurred and the mayor and others signed off on it. Voelker assured me that no board I did not like or want would be placed above me. I expressed some doubt about that but said I thought a good board was always a strong idea.

I said, "I will think about this," and the meeting ended.

As I left the restaurant, my ears were burning. Move the federal funds to another organization outside the purview of the city council? Get the White House involved in diverting funds from duly authorized local government entities? I sent the mayor an email outlining the conversation and expressing my dismay.

This wouldn't be the end of NORA's attempts to hijack the recovery.

A few weeks later, in April, I made a presentation to the LRA board, and at its conclusion, one of the members raised the issue of setting up a new vehicle—outside city government—to handle the recovery money. He asked point blank if the recovery might be handled better by such a group.

I replied that there were perhaps five or six people who had experience in running recoveries from disasters such as Katrina. Since I was one of them, I declared that if the intention was to have someone else handle the funds, then I would go home.

The meeting chairman skillfully shut down further discussion. As I walked out, a *Times-Picayune* reporter came up to interview me. I told him firmly that if I wasn't going run the recovery, there was no reason for me to stay in New Orleans.

On the way back to my house in the car, Duce remarked, "Doc, I heard what you said in there. Turn around. I need to see the back of your suit. People here don't talk back like you did. I think you just put a big bullseye on your back."

I would soon learn that he was right. This was my first bullseye, with more to come.

Charges and countercharges flew back and forth between NORA and other outspoken groups on how to proceed with the recovery money. In early April, I made a statement that became infamous, calling some of those characters "buffoons." My comments, which appeared in a *New York Times* interview, outraged the *Times-Picayune*, which broadened the statement to include all New

Orleanians even though it was clear that I meant only a narrow group that I was battling with, who were more interested in controlling money than spearheading a sound recovery.

Over the next month, May, I worked with my staff to develop a program to devote all *city* funds that legally could be used for the purpose to recovery projects. I needed to do this so no one could claim that we didn't know where the recovery money was going to be spent, as NORA was alleging. This approach formed the backbone of our recovery-financing program. Using it, we tracked progress and spending in each target area. My reasoning was simple: I knew that I had to get the money flowing into the neighborhoods, or continue to face these assaults on the recovery by NORA and others. We devised a six-part budget-tracking program:

1. We refocused federal funds for community recovery. For example, Community Development Block Grants, which amounted to about $15 million annually for housing and community services, were reoriented to the target areas wherever possible.
2. We redeployed about $40 million in city funds that came from special taxes and normally would have been spent on economic development.
3. Since we had floated a bond fund, we used these funds to match the recovery areas so that bond-funded street paving and community center improvements would be spent in the same places where FEMA funds were being used for the restoration of fire stations or other public buildings. This amounted to almost $300 million, part of that money from older bond issues whose proceeds were unspent prior to the storm.
4. We found that the state bond commission had no guidelines for using post-Katrina federal GO Bond funds. As a result, the money was going to oil companies that had suffered no damage, and cities that had experienced only a little. We wrote guidelines and asked the state to allocate a pool of funds solely for New Orleans projects that met our recovery objectives.
5. My staff, led by lead planner Dubravka Gilic, devised a $417 million LRA City of New Orleans Recovery Community Development plan, broken down as follows: $200 million-plus to neighborhood recovery; $100 million to new economic development; and the remainder to arts, culture, and education.

TABLE 2

Funding source amount	Budgeted ($)
LRA-Obligated Recovery Funds (D-CDBG)	410,720,016*
Traditional CDBG grants	42,925,126
UDAG funds	16,562,252**
HOME investment grants	16,340,133***
FEMA (PA funds)	11,236,931
EDF grants	10,931,124***
Other governmental grants	9,388,962***
NHIF grants	6,804,932***
General fund	4,484,794
BRAC grants	460,258**
Other nongovernmental grants	75,000
Total	529,854,528

Source: ORDA 2008.
*Long-term community development funds different from traditional CDBG grants.
**City and federal funds not associated with disaster.
***City funds from taxes or related sources.

6. I identified the federal and state agencies that were operating in New Orleans after the storm, for example: Department of Commerce Small Business Administration; Treasury Department community programs; Department of Housing and Urban Development; and Louisiana's Housing Finance Agency. Then I requested of their local representatives that they allocate the money they were planning to spend in New Orleans primarily to our target areas. The agencies cooperated with us because, in most cases, they had no better way to meet their objectives.

We had a plan, an administrative system, and a budget. But having a plan and a budget would make little difference if we couldn't alter the social and economic conditions for the people most affected by the storm and by prior years of economic and social deprivation. I had to start a process that would alter the economic stakes, too.

I began pondering ideas for rebuilding New Orleans's economy, and a bridge across the economic divide between black and white; downtown and the neighborhoods.

9. REVIVING A DROWNING ECONOMY

KNOWLEDGEABLE POLICY SCHOLARS ARGUED OPENLY THAT perhaps New Orleans had little economic reason to live.

Leading policy economist Ed Glasser, in a piece he described as a "thought experiment," which I learned about in my first visit to Harvard in 2007, said that with the federal government pledging billions of dollars in aid, most of which never materialized, people would be better off not thinking about a place-based strategy that emphasized cash payments to residents. Instead, they could choose to use the cash to reinvest in whatever living arrangements they had in the city, or to relocate to Atlanta, Houston, or any other place they might want to go.

When I visited Harvard in April 2007 to enlist allies for the recovery effort, several professors and students asked openly if we should perhaps let cities like New Orleans die and move on, given the cost associated with rebuilding a dying city. As one student observed, New Orleans exudes nostalgia but has virtually no economic value to the nation. She noted that towns have come and gone throughout U.S. history. Dodge City was important in the early cattle rush; California, along with much of the West, is littered with places that died or shrank—in California's case, after the Gold Rush—along with their physical and economic fortunes. Clearly, New Orleans has more attributes than these earlier examples. But they were once important places, too. So why not let New Orleans die?

Arguments over the city's economic and social value continue. Robert Lang, one of the leading scholars of regional economics, asserts that New Orleans belongs to a larger zone that stretches from Houston to Pensacola, Florida. Within that zone, New Orleans dominated until the 1950s, when the techno-

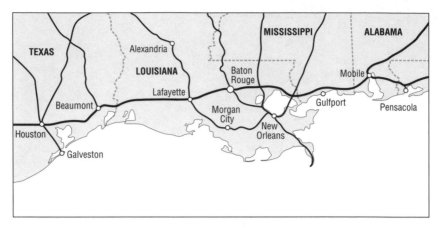

logical innovation of container ships led to the diversion of seagoing traffic to Mobile and Houston, and New Orleans declined as a port city.

In the process, New Orleans began a larger, gradual economic decline from a premier national city to an appendage of Houston. Major firms in the oil and related extraction industries decamped to neighboring cities, lured by their modern ports and superior financial and service infrastructures of lawyers, banks, and accounting firms. Houston used its political clout in the Lyndon Johnson era to garner federal facilities to support its growing labor force. New Orleans slipped economically as major cities around it grew.

Mobile gained seaport business at New Orleans's expense. The city's regional medical preeminence also waned. In the 1940s and 1950s, New Orleans boasted world-class medical facilities, serving not only the South but also the Caribbean, Central America, and the northern coast of South America. The Charity Hospital System guaranteed state dollars to support high-quality medical teaching. (The strength of the Charity System is also its weakness: years of direct support for the hospital from Louisiana allowed the LSU medical teaching faculty to rely on sinecures while nearby states and nations in the Caribbean and elsewhere developed new, competitive medical infrastructures.) Meanwhile, Birmingham was building a solid education-medical economy, destined to propel it past New Orleans as the Southern medical hub.

The last civic insult came in the musical area. The city that from the turn of the twentieth century had presented itself to the world as the home of jazz lost its musical production and distribution business to Memphis, Atlanta, and Miami. New Orleans had made almost no investments in modern performance infrastructure to match those more entrepreneurial rivals. New Orleans instead drifted into a tourism-dominated economy based on low wages, public housing, and public assistance. When Katrina hit, the median income of the New Orleans region was just *half* the national figure. Even lower African American median incomes and occupational profiles had made the city one of the poorest in the nation before Katrina.

As New Orleans lost its economic position locally, regionally, and globally, and nearby rivals took bold actions to secure their own, the city became embroiled in defending its past. Civic groups tried the great leap forward by proposing a 1984 New Orleans World's Fair, but the idea was undermined by the newspapers and civic elites. In any case, the fair would have been an image builder, not a genuine economic development tool. Other endeavors to revitalize the economy emerged in the "model cities" of the 1970s with downtown malls and stadiums. Meanwhile, such central assets as the Mississippi River, educational and medical facilities, and positioning of a high-tech base at the Michaud space complex gained little support. Pre-Katrina New Orleans was simply a tourist town.

When I arrived there, I gave one of my first speeches to a citywide audience after looking at those economic trends and data. I said the city had a tee-shirt economy that purchased the beads for Mardi Gras from China, and virtually all its food, except some fish, from neighboring states, and that Katrina presented the opportunity to rebuild the entire economy, not just houses and city buildings. I explained that major disasters alter local economies forever.

I cited Kobe, Japan, as an illustration. Prior to the 1995 earthquake, Kobe was one of the top three steel-exporting ports in the world. But five years after the quake it was not even among the top 25. In my own hometown, Oakland, the 1989 earthquake presented an opportunity to move the 880 Freeway that ran along the east side of San Francisco Bay toward the Port of Oakland. Doing so eased truck traffic to the port, relocated rail lines, and improved the size of the city's seaport since the city bought army and navy bases to create a larger, intermodal transport system that I'd recommended. (In fact, I'd recommended all those actions to the mayor and the city's port commission before the earthquake.)

I also told the mayor, council, and business leaders at the meeting that the revitalization of post-September 11 Lower Manhattan was proposed by Robert Yaro, president of the Regional Plan Association, and myself soon after the attacks, and that the plan, which included altering the Lower Manhattan transport links and rebuilding the civic, residential, and "amenities" base on Manhattan's West side, was already well underway.

In other talks with civic leaders, I advocated that the recovery aim at the city's economic infrastructure, in order to position the economy nationally and globally. I was openly critical of the existing employment structure, and I also proposed a program of economic and social justice. In addition, I said in various presentations that we shouldn't create jobs for the future without preparing locals to fill them.

For at least three years before I came to New Orleans, the Regional Planning Commission had been engaged in serious studies to form a biomedical complex in the central city area. This was just the sort of initiative that fit with my ideas for the city's economic infrastructure. The medical assets were already at hand: the Louisiana State University School of Medicine, Tulane School of Medicine, Veterans Administration (VA) Hospital, Ochsner Health Foundation, Xavier School of Pharmacy, Charity Hospital (the clinical practice hospital for LSU Medicine), and—planned for the same part of the city—a state-of-the-art Louisiana Cancer Center. From Sydney, I reviewed documents sent to me by the Regional Planning staff. An official at the Regional Planning Commission invited me on a tour of St. Louis to see how that city's new VA facility was transforming a community with a demographic like that of New Orleans.

I couldn't make the tour, but Addkison represented Mayor Nagin, and she returned enthusiastic about New Orleans's plan for a biomedical complex. Impressed with its potential to boost economic development, she took the lead in promoting the complex. Because I had given biomed a central position in the recovery strategy I was articulating, I was happy to support her efforts.

When I attended a planning meeting, however, it quickly became clear that planning wasn't progressing well.

As in St. Louis, a VA hospital was scheduled for inclusion in the New Orleans biomedical venture. Representing the VA at our meeting was a smart, articulate woman named Julie Catellier. She pushed for the city to take a proactive and decisive role in assembling the land and infrastructure so that the VA could locate its hospital near the proposed new LSU facility. The new hospital, she pointed out, didn't have to be *in* New Orleans—a dire statement that drew gasps from the LSU, Tulane, and Regional Planning staff in attendance. Several people asked Addkison what the city could and should do to make sure the VA stayed and got built in downtown New Orleans. Addkison sidestepped this issue by pointing out that the city was engaged in a massive recovery effort with little or no cash to spare.

At that point, council member Stacy Head turned to me and asked, exasperated, "How would you handle this, Dr. Blakely?" I responded by laying out a several-point approach that seemed logical from the documents I'd read. I wanted the city to take the lead by offering to purchase whatever land was required, to provide the infrastructure for the VA, including water and parking, and to secure surrounding areas for future development. At that point, the momentum of the meeting swung to me as the facilitator. Although we worked together and theoretically were on the same team, Addkison told the assembled group that my ideas wouldn't work because, as she had just said, there was no money and the mayor hadn't authorized an effort of this size.

The pivotal issue was who would buy the land for the VA hospital to relocate next to LSU. The agency had funds to build the facility but traditionally had asked localities to provide land. Adding to the complication of the project for me was the fact that the storm-damaged old VA hospital occupied a site too small for a new proposed hospital for vets. So the VA had three choices: find a better site in the New Orleans region; leave for Florida, where land was available and free; or pursue an open competition for all areas in the South or near the LSU's proposed medical research-hospital complex.

I suggested that the state take the lead in assembling the land for the joint LSU-VA campus. Because the state possessed stronger eminent domain authority than the city, it could handle the land acquisition for the VA, making the reimbursements later. I asked, "Why not a joint enterprise—with the state acting as the original purchaser of the needed land, and the city as a partner?"

Addkison opposed this idea on several grounds. For one thing, she argued, the city lacked the funds; for another, the state would never agree to act as a proxy for the city.

Other participants, however, liked the idea. The VA rep reminded us that her agency planned to issue a Request of Interest for parties to bid on locations in the New Orleans area. As she put it, "This is not a done deal for New Orleans." Those assembled agreed to present my proposal to the mayor and the council.

A week later, I put the idea on the mayor's executive agenda, after taking the precaution of speaking with the state authorities about the basic concept. (I enlisted their support, but imposed many caveats.) The executive staff meeting didn't lead to a decision, but it did reveal that the mayor had reservations similar to Addkison's. I countered with a plea to look at alternative financing for the project, including issuing GO Zone bonds or Community Development Block Grant funds, if we received a larger allocation of the latter than the feds originally allocated. I argued that there would almost be a second round of CDBG money for the city, and that this project was a logical and ideal way to spend it. We couldn't risk having the VA leave downtown or, worse, go to another state.

Based on my knowledge, research, and writing on economic development, I also put to Nagin and his team an argument for using the VA as the anchor for the city's economic recovery. Hospitals import new capital from other places in the state and nation. The VA hospital serves seven states, bringing in patients for days, weeks, or months. These patients come with families who occupy local hotels and buy local goods and services. In addition, the hospital both buys and sells services across the nation as it develops medical specialties, such as burn therapy. Moreover, with LSU and Tulane's teaching and research hospitals, the new complex planned to specialize in tropical diseases and health, which would bring in millions of dollars in new research funds and attract patients from Latin America and Africa. The mayor, warming to the idea, reminded me that until the 1980s the LSU-Tulane complex was the prime health care venue for well-to-do Latin American and Caribbean patients. When the deal was finally reached, the mayor picked up on the research angle and repeatedly cited the fact that the VA system had spawned three Nobel prizes in medicine. He said that he intended to have the next few prize winners in New Orleans.

Soon afterward, with the city attorney, chief administrative officer, finance director, and others in attendance, I made my case again. This time the mayor liked it. But Addkison had one last card to play. The state, she said, would never agree to what I was proposing. I suggested that Nagin call the Louisiana director of facilities and ask him directly if he would become the city's partner.

With the phone on speaker, Jerry Jones, head of state facilities, came on the line.

The mayor put the proposition to him.

I held my breath, until I heard Jerry drawl, "I think we can do that, Mr. Mayor."

A major battle was at last over, and my side had won.

Now that she'd lost, Addkison got with the program quickly. She and her team fashioned a Memorandum of Understanding (MOU) with the state in record time. The request for interest appeared in the newspaper a few days later. Addkison and the Regional Planning Commission team put together a response.

We were on good terms with the Ochsner Foundation, one of New Orleans's major healthcare providers, and we knew that Ochsner had a suitable site for our project right in the area. The head of the hospital informed the mayor that the biggest healthcare provider in New Orleans and maybe the state was determined to put its new facility right on the Ochsner campus to capture the GI patient load and staff. Although that sounded good to my colleagues, I took a contrary view. Siting the new facility at the downtown location proposed by the city would have the highest direct economic impact on the people of New Orleans, and was therefore preferable to what the foundation was offering.

I stood up, thanked the group a second time, and headed for the exit.

Duce was aghast. "Doc," he said, "you know what you just did?! I told you once already, you don't do that here. Not to people like that. Now you got *another* target on your back. You don't have much more room *left* on your back. This is the only hospital in town that's fully operational." Then he gave me a big high five, and we drove off.

Less than a week later, I got a telephone call from the office of the secretary of the VA. Andy Love, special assistant to the secretary, said that the city proposal needed clarification, and offered to come to see me. He flew in, and we closeted ourselves for almost a day to go over the city offer. He made clear he was calling on others to clarify their proposals as well.

For the next six weeks, Andy and I engaged in intense negotiations. I was assigned a city attorney, who took the job on as one of his most important legal challenges. He and I stayed in the office until late at night, hammering out the specifics on:

- What land, located where?
- How to deal with historic buildings
- Site clearance responsibilities
- Utilities
- Environmental requirements
- Delivery dates
- Transfer of the storm-damaged VA hospital after building a new VA adjacent to LSU
- Penalties for nonperformance

Thanks to my background in land assembly as a developer with my own firm and my work with the City of Oakland, the city attorney's skills, and Andy Love's flexibility, we produced a draft agreement that the mayor and state representatives signed.

Duce was all smiles. "Watch your back, Doc," he said, "and don't get sick."

I was energized by our accomplishments with the state. But I knew this battle wasn't over. I had to find the money to buy the land and deal with the strong emotional and environmental concerns about the maintenance of Charity Hospital. Charity was the place many New Orleaneans were born, and if you were poor the only hospital that would take you.

■ ■ ■

Of course, the city's economic recovery depended on more than a hospital complex, however important the VA agreement.

With that in mind, I next turned my attention to the reestablishment of New Orleans as an exporter of music and performing arts. That meant establishing the city as a digital performance center with optical and high-bandwidth venues. The backbone of the approach was to make Canal Street what I called in speeches the "Digital Canal." The important Mahalia Jackson Performance Center was to be transformed into a modern venue to support all forms of live and recorded performance at one end of the downtown. And at the Saenger Theater, anchoring the other end of the downtown, creative city CDBG financing would produce a venue for live drama and music, which would bring back the creative heart of the city—with the large hospital staff, and patients with their families, as year-round patrons.

My rationale was simple. We could have fulltime, not episodic, visitors who would need places to be entertained. But stadiums and similar projects, like the expansion of the Superdome, are not economic generators. They don't bring in new money, because the people who attend the games are locals, so they're only transferring their entertainment dollars from a local theater or night club to the stadium, with no net gain of money for the city and region.

We also expanded the Michaud Mars Lander project, the next-generation spacecraft, because making new space rockets requires a whole bunch of sustainable products. New Orleans needed to leapfrog into the future, using solar ventures and related technologies with potential spin-off industries that could contribute to rebuilding our housing and repaving our streets. In addition to the sun, wind, and Mississippi River waters driving new energy sources, I reasoned that all the new firms could be staffed from scientists at Michaud, the city's seven universities, or elsewhere in the community.

To support a new technology approach, we had to upgrade a city infrastructure that in some cases hadn't been touched for over fifty years. For example, road maintenance was poor, because the city is sinking, and there were few records of facility maintenance.

To start the upgrade process, I located a small group of dedicated individuals, including Doug Meffert of Tulane University. He understood that revamping the basic infrastructure—using advanced techniques and materials for a low-carbon future—fit well with the sciences being developed at Tulane and other city universities. So we invested in smart-technology revitalization projects on the New Orleans waterfront, especially in those that would provide energy from the river.

Another tool we used to help modernize the city economically was the GO Zone bond. The GO Zone legislation aimed at getting larger scale, job-producing businesses back in operation as soon as possible after the storm. GO Zone bonds were provided at low interest rates with long paybacks, and the state had considerable latitude in allocating them. They were not without complications. Rules stipulated that eligible firms had to be located in damaged areas, but not that a particular *firm* had experienced any damage. Moreover, the bonds could only go to large private companies able to sustain the legal and underwriting costs for a bond issue, and to float the issue on public markets. State rules didn't require endorsement from local governments, except for perfunctory acknowledgments by the local business Enterprise Corporation, and large-scale organizations even managed to bypass that modest requirement.

One day in early November 2007, a staff member brought me a document showing applications for GO Zone bonds in New Orleans. Alarms sounded—not for the first time since I'd been the recovery czar. Although we had only a few applicants, the state was approaching the total ceiling for its bond allocations. More disconcertingly, large organizations barely damaged in areas lightly hit by flooding were getting most of them. Meanwhile, in New Orleans, we thought we had to have a recovery plan before we applied for GO Zone bonds.

With Kenya Smith leading the way, we reconsidered the process, and wound up establishing workable bond criteria. Then the mayor called the state treasurer to argue for a fair allocation and a rollback of the projects that didn't meet the criteria and specifically target New Orleans. Within a few weeks, our staff had developed projects for the state bond commission based on our Target Area Plan. The state bond commission modified criteria for proposed projects that looked like ours in New Orleans. One of the new criteria required that organizations proposing projects had actually suffered storm damage, or were closely tied to the economic recovery of the community where the project would be located.

This commitment and the modified criteria became the template for the bond commission, and the state treasurer gave me time early and often to argue my points before the group. As part of our revolving fund for rebuilding, we negotiated a bond allocation that matched the appraised value of the old VA site. The city would enter a 99-year lease of the old site to pay back the bond.

I had a personal charge: to create a system that would quickly get and spend the money needed to put some cranes on the skyline.

PART III

Elements of the City

THANKS TO ITS MUSIC, NEW ORLEANS IS JUSTIFIABLY KNOWN as the "soul city." But if the term "soul" is taken to mean "soul-mate," as in the sharing of a common identity and sense of directions and goals, then New Orleans falls far short of the mark. New Orleanians frequently use soul to refer to the collective spirit of the city. The city has a spirit, but it lacks manifestations of it that foster cohesion.

According to research by Lawrence Vale and Thomas Campanella in *The Resilient City*, among the most important tools in a disaster recovery is a city's cohesiveness, which helps create a purpose and a vision of restoration from the collective trauma. Vale and Campanella show that organizations that are strong before or after the disaster are an essential component for a speedy recovery.

Civic organizations like those the researchers discuss exist in some U.S. cities that have experienced great calamities, such as San Francisco after the 1906 earthquake, and Chicago after the Great Fire of 1871. These events brought both cities new strengths that they used to forge a path to the future. In each case, an organization that transcended local politics was in place to lead the recoveries and to shape the road ahead. Such organizations have a purpose beyond the event. They are civic, not political, institutions, but they are the seed bed of sociopolitical organization. Mayors and council members in many cases have emerged from them, bringing to government a citywide agenda forged over many years.

Although New Orleans has a plethora of organizations, none act as the central resource for carrying a civic vision. By contrast, the San Francisco Planning + Urban Research Association (SPUR) epitomizes the kind of entity needed for recovery: civic-led and financially independent of government. SPUR played a leading role in reshaping its city after the 1989 earthquake. Across the Bay, a similar group, Oakland Sharing the Vision, arose after the same event to play a similar role for that city.

New Orleans's many civic organizations coalesce along political, church, and ethnic lines, and the krewes that form the backbone of the Mardi Gras parades. But almost none of those groups represent a broad, cross-racial constituency with a common destiny. One of my professor colleagues at Berkeley described a certain dilemma of urban planning as follows: "A person or a group of people can be looking down a street. One focusing north and the other south, they will swear that on the same street, they see different things because they face opposite directions. Both groups believe they are the only ones seeing the truth and they won't accept any other view."

That is New Orleans, in spades. Everybody has his or her own version of truth, but fails to see or respect the other versions, because he's looking in only one direction.

An important, and vexing, actor among the city's fractured associations was the influential Bureau of Governmental Research (BGR), which views itself as the local government watchdog. It selects issues it feels are being inadequately dealt with by the city council, and interviews senior staff about them. My staff did their best to try to correct BGR's misapprehensions, but found they were talking to people whose minds were made up or who simply didn't know how government works.

For their part, many local black leaders, unfortunately, see the BGR as a white organization. No matter who chairs it (and some blacks have done so), the organization, in the African American view, is staffed by whites who consistently criticize a black city government. There's been truth in that perception. The BGR has no representation or standing with the vast number of lower-income blacks, or with the black community in general, on issues such as ending job inequality and combating overt racial discrimination in private clubs. The BGR, I was told more than once by black activists, existed solely to bring down the black city government. In my view, the BGR is a criticizer. It didn't take advantage of its opportunity to also be a healer, which is what's needed in a post-disaster situation.

As recovery director I spent several months trying to find or create some group that might fill the void and carry a long-term civic message, build coalitions, and groom leadership. To be sure, well-intentioned organizations did appear. But each of them carved out a narrow mandate. I asked my friend

Steven Bingler, a well-known and highly regarded architect who crossed racial and political lines, to convene a meeting with community leaders of a kindred spirit to see if we could mold some overarching cross-color civic organization.

I worked with the Horizon Initiative, a middle-income, post-Katrina group that pledged to alter the economic direction of the city with a new public-private partnership. I championed Horizon, even when many thought the organization an interloper on the civic agenda and wanted to take away its access to public funds. Council member Arnie Fielkow's strong support of Horizon became a racial issue, because he's white.

Other grassroots groups arose in communities across the city after the storm, but they had little in common. As a result, such groups seldom had strong, if any, representation in places like the lower Ninth Ward or Central City. New Orleans East built its own coalitions, which suffered many internal conflicts. My remark to the *New York Times* about Sunni- and Shiite-like hostilities among these factions sparked outrage. When I later appeared on the black radio station WBOK to discuss the recovery, call-in listeners agreed with my observations, wholeheartedly thanking me for having the courage to voice them.

For most African Americans, leadership on civic agendas had to come from City Hall's black elected leaders; black *community* leadership was too fragmented or divided to provide it. Consequently, too many African American community leaders' quests for political and economic strength focused their attention on City Hall.

Many residential, community-based groups formed either just before or just after the storm to protect physical and social space. In most cases, they pursued parochial projects. I was impressed by the spirit and dedicated leadership of many of the groups. Nonetheless, most saw their opportunities in reference to others as a zero-sum game. When I mentioned to a white elected official the need to tilt resources to the Ninth Ward, she replied, "I've never been there, so why would we do that?!" She was echoing other whites I spoke to about that neighborhood's plight and its need for citywide attention. One of them, an angry Tulane University student from a town near New Orleans, challenged me in an open forum: "Why should we put the city at risk for those people?"—meaning residents of the Ninth.

This us-against-them attitude left low-income communities feeling that they had to grab and secure resources before any citywide goals could be formulated. Blacks viewed community coalitions such as BNOB as yet more attempts to rid New Orleans of low-income blacks and make it the Las Vegas of the South. Some of the black anger over giving the city master plan the force of law stemmed from the belief that the plan would prove to be what a black former state legislator called the "final solution," aimed at eliminating or marginalizing his people the way prewar Germany treated Jews in the Warsaw ghetto. He suggested publicly that the white community's determination to exclude black neighborhoods would be etched into planning law.

The New Orleans post-Katrina landscape, a toxic soup that covered the city for more than two months, spawned environmental and green groups that were a positive force across the city. I supported their agendas to make New Orleans a safer place to live and work. But these groups were composed of true believers. And although they tended to be more racially diverse, they weren't ideologically varied, and they seldom reached out to support other causes, such as historic preservation, that seemed to be their natural allies.

An organization called Women of the Storm did forge some relationships across the ranks of upper-class blacks and whites who shared an interest in the survival of their city. "Women" didn't have a race agenda. On its face, that was a good thing; however, without a deliberate agenda that healed the rifts between blacks and whites, they weren't able to meet their own aspirations. They tried desperately to get the 2008 presidential debates held in New Orleans but lost out to, of all places, the much smaller Oxford, Mississippi. The committee reasoned that New Orleans wasn't yet ready to host the debates, even after it had already hosted the All-Star basketball game and several football bowl games, and even though the Convention Center was undamaged. Certainly, New Orleans had more hotel beds than Oxford, Mississippi. I suspect that perceptions of crime were the real reasons, and they can't be swept under the rug, as my grandma liked to say.

The city council saw itself as a community-advocacy organization to make municipal systems work better. But race divided the common agenda, and understandably so: black council members rightly or wrongly saw increased city services to impoverished areas as the way to level the playing field, while whites saw as their mandate the equal *dispersal* of services. Several white members openly expressed their frustration, calling city projects "pork barrels" for black contractors.

Nearly every try at building a civic coalition turned on the simplistic notion that the current mayor needed to improve his performance or a new one had to be elected. I likened this to the "cargo cult" delusion—a reference to Pacific aboriginal tribes that built small runways near their villages, thinking

Building site.
Author's photograph

that that would cause cargo planes with food to land, and end their poverty. So, too, in New Orleans, whatever ailed the city, from bad streets to black poverty, would somehow disappear with a new mayor.

Although good mayors do good things, few can overcome all the problems in their cities. Good mayors even get voted out of office despite doing fine deeds, simply because many problems lie beyond governmental purview or solution. Mayor Rudolph Giuliani is often credited with turning New York City around. But his success owed a considerable amount to actions taken by many civic organizations in the city.

Several meetings I organized to promote a wider civic vision were derailed when Mayor Nagin became the target of scapegoating and vicious attacks, including a charge of corruption. I tended to try to steer these discussions to what could be achieved, not discussing what the current or future mayor might do.

Trying to combat a semi-messianic notion that the "right" mayor would *make* it all right, I pointed out how few issues that affect daily lives are actually controlled by the mayor. A New Orleans mayor doesn't deliver water or power or deal with the meager budgets for street repairs or antipoverty initiatives. As in most American cities, 80 to 90 percent of the New Orleans budget goes to fund police and fire and related essential services.

I knew from my experience with two mayors that not much change comes with a new black mayor or a new white mayor. The local institutional direction and budgets are too firmly fixed. Mayors have at most 10 to 15 percent of the city budget as discretionary; the rest is in police and fire and pensions. I finally allowed matters to take their own course and stopped trying to forge new approaches to a civic direction.

Civic associations weren't easy to forge or find in New Orleans—but in disaster recovery generally, I believe that they are indeed a critical element. As Vale and Campanella write in their *Axioms of Resilience*, "The process of rebuilding is a necessary but, by itself, insufficient condition for enabling recovery. . . . Cities are more than a sum of their buildings. They are also a thick concatenation of social and cultural matter. To enable recovery . . . networks must be reconnected."

11. MORE THAN BRICKS AND STICKS: REVIVING NEIGHBORHOODS

ON MY MANY BIKE EXPEDITIONS AROUND NEW ORLEANS AS the Bicycle Guy, I got to see the city's residents as neighbors, and in neighborhoods. Some places suffered little storm damage but had large-scale problems that predated the storm, such as dilapidated houses and neglected streetscapes. I saw that income was and is a dividing factor, but not entirely so: a larger determinant of a neighborhood's viability appeared to be the mix of people who were committed to making the neighborhood a stronger community after Katrina than before.

The residents of Broadmoor and Lakeview, for example, had neighborhood survival characteristics. They asked for little and did a lot for themselves. Interestingly, as a result, these communities became the target of abuse by others who perceived them as getting more than their share of city government attention and assistance. Years of corruption had bred suspicion that if you paid off city officials, your community would receive favored treatment.

Some places, such as the Ninth Ward, whose travails received the most media coverage, got help from church groups nationwide. I observed that the more help they received from the outside in the form of volunteers, the more they expected from both the outside volunteers and the city. For two consecutive weekends, city staff did an energetic sweep in New Orleans East. Working side by side with local volunteers from the area, we fixed up and cleaned up. We removed truckloads of trash and mowed lawns. Three weeks later, I got irate calls from several residents, saying that we needed to come back. The weeds, they complained, were continuing to grow. When I asked the callers if *they* could do some of the work, they responded, "We get around town. We see how you keep up those other neighborhoods!"

My biggest contribution to New Orleans neighborhoods, before we got any money for the communities, was to ride my bike into them and bolster the residents' resolve. Although the trips gave *me* more information, that was little solace for the people who had waited years for any sign of federal help. I took my share of hostile comments for failing to get the money delivered faster. Federal Community Block Grant funds are by law restricted to neighborhood renewal and similar objectives, so any federal recovery funds using community block money had to meet this test.

We received little money from FEMA to repair our neighborhood police and fire stations. The city had to take $30 million from its tight budget to repair vital facilities quickly—with no assurance that this huge amount would ever be reimbursed. In other recoveries I've worked on, the state or FEMA advanced the funds so that vital facilities could get up and running again.

My observation of the help President Bush sent was that neither Donald Powell, Bush's first Katrina emissary to New Orleans, nor his second one, Donald O'Dell, was very interested in representing us to Washington or trying to get things done for the city. Powell spent most of his time meeting with non-city or non-state people on what seemed like local political issues. O'dell considered his mission to be making the city's new requests better organized and articulated, rather than getting the long list of previous requests even looked at by FEMA or other agencies.

Moreover, my colleagues at FEMA who had worked with me earlier in Oakland were very candid and told me it was best to come directly to them because they didn't report to Powell, and they were even more emphatic about that directive after O'dell assumed the same role. It was clear that there was more than a little bureaucratic infighting going on as to who was in charge.

I pushed for an independent assessment of our FEMA claims, and Senator Mary Landrieu got that done, but with no assistance from anyone at the White House.

I found that I had much better results going directly to FEMA, HUD, and the Environmental Protection Agency (EPA), either on my own or with delegates from the other parishes, to get funds for neighborhoods and housing. Senator Landrieu's office was very sympathetic to our plight and worked with us. Curiously, just before I left New Orleans, the senator's office came down hard on the mayor and city for underspending HUD funds, even though that was easily explained and, within a few months, cleared up; it seemed like some kind of political punch at the mayor. I was also targeted, but it was hard to blame me, because the alleged underspending had almost all occurred before Katrina or before my coming into office. HUD staffers told me that most of Louisiana had similar underspending problems.

The issue of the "right to return" was very heated. Underlying it was the fact that many New Orleans residents who couldn't return were underinsured or living in public housing or senior citizen facilities. Economic realities and demography made promises to return more than a little shallow. Many Ninth Ward residents were over seventy, and the idea of rebuilding didn't appeal to them.

Our response was to build good senior housing, using our HUD funds, so that seniors who *could* return had decent places to live. In my two years in office, thanks to the many strong church and nonprofit providers, we opened several hundred new and rebuilt senior facilities.

All the same, the prospects of returning were daunting. A number of factors are important in understanding who could or might return. Seniors and people with low incomes were at an inherent disadvantage in a system that required rebuilding houses. Low-income residents were also dependent on government supports and transfers, and thus not in a position to take out a new mortgage or supervise home rebuilding. This left them vulnerable to exploitation. One of the saddest duties I faced daily was taking calls and reading letters from seniors ripped off by unscrupulous contractors. In addition, seniors with resources might not have felt it worthwhile to embark on a rebuilding project at an advanced age. They might have elected instead to find a smaller place or stay with relatives.

Cheap rental housing was plentiful prior to the storm. Owners who left the city just wanted someone on the property. Before the storm New Orleans had many small-time landlords who bought abandoned or distressed housing as rental units. Post-Katrina, however, the cost of rebuilding these places exceeded the rents owners could command, so they just let the places fall apart. The state had a good small-owner program; but like so many of these efforts, in my view, it was designed to prevent fraud rather than get houses built. The paperwork was too burdensome for small landlords. So the units that were rebuilt were expensive by pre-storm standards, and that, too, had the effect of keeping people from returning.

An investment in rebuilding is a financial and psychological burden. People returned to their neighborhoods much faster than predicted. But with the memories of the devastation still fresh, many just couldn't face the prospect of rebuilding. Many others simply didn't get enough from the Road Home program to consider doing so.

There is general agreement that, when I left in 2009, the New Orleans population stood at about 330,000 or a bit more. The official population according to the 2010 Census is 343,829. About 30 percent or more are newcomers or born after the storm, according to reports by the Brookings Institution. That's a strong rebound, considering the depth of the Katrina tragedy and the listless attempts to attract the lowest-income residents back to the city.

Due to the impediments to return, the city's demographic base has changed. The new residents are younger and better educated than the former residential base. New Orleans is now a place for pioneers. Brookings reports found many newcomers cashing in on the tide of new construction and related jobs.

But construction and labor jobs didn't materialize for many unemployed and underemployed blacks. Post-Katrina opportunity structures in construction haven't yielded as many good, new jobs for blacks. Many current residents see Latinos as poachers, since skilled Latinos seeking work came in from Texas and Mexico as soon as the water levels went down. So by the time blacks started pushing for more jobs, they were outnumbered and outcompeted by lower cost outside labor. In some cases, lack of skills actually was the problem. But when I asked local black workers about that in community meetings, they'd say the "big boys" were keeping them out of work. Employers preferred Latinos, they contended, because they wouldn't complain about wages or working conditions. At the many sites I visited, few had more than a handful of blacks on the job.

On one hand, therefore, things were looking better for New Orleans. New people tend to attract or create new jobs. The city's burgeoning graphics, media, and information industries illustrate the value of an influx of human skills. On the other hand, the rebound in neighborhoods wasn't shared equally by all New Orleanians.

The arts scene, as well as the cultural one, was always much deeper and stronger in New Orleans than the national press depicted, and an anchor, or potential anchor, for other neighborhoods. Bourbon Street and its environs have created a culturally shallow stereotype of New Orleans debauchery. Image and reality in New Orleans are badly skewed by the constant presentation in the media and tourism materials of youthful wild drinking as the epicenter, the sine qua non, of the city. But this city was the second place in North America to host European opera. The ballet, symphony, and theater, traditionally strong, revived right after the storm, thanks to Tulane University and churches offering the use of their facilities.

It was once reported that I seldom attended New Orleans events and that

I was aloof from goings-on in the city. In fact, I spent many weekends pursuing cultural activities. True, I seldom went to Bourbon Street. But I did attend every major classical artistic performance time permitted. I made the rebuilding of the Mahalia Jackson Performance Center a personal priority. Cynthia Sylvain-Lear, deputy city administrator, led that effort, and I urged our project management contractor, MWH, to help make it a reality. I found good companionship among local Jackson Theater aficionados, too.

I used City Park Museum to host official events. It's an incredible asset to the entire region. There, I met many people who were volunteering or on the museum staff, and I've kept in touch with several of them.

The social space for artists in New Orleans is much larger and more eclectic than that in many parts of the nation. That said, rivalries among arts groups such as competing jazz organizations made donations and other support difficult for them collectively.

Cities and neighborhoods need arts and culture, but for me the basic need was the restoration of the health and education systems. No project took more of my energy than Methodist Hospital in New Orleans East. This over-200-bed hospital served its neighborhood and much of the eastern part of the central city. Methodist, a private for-profit health care center, was so badly damaged by the hurricane that the owners decided not to reopen it.

Prior to the storm, the hospital complex had been thriving. But the owners, Universal Health Care of Philadelphia, had to deal with the prospect of reopening in a region with a shrinking overall population and in an environment where all local hospitals were facing difficult financial challenges.

But the hospital was a key economic anchor in the heart of the community. It was adjacent to a subregional shopping center, and the two commercial facilities were synergistic, since the hospital brought doctors and healthcare staff who shopped at the center, and this, in turn, brought local residents as shoppers. So loss of the hospital was more than a healthcare issue: there was a real danger of dragging down the entire New Orleans East neighborhood economy if the hospital wasn't rebuilt.

New Orleans East community groups were outraged by the hospital owners' action, and demanded that the city and the mayor do something about it. I sided with the community, and visited Universal Health Care headquarters to offer a number of alternative proposals. Placing the city at risk in owning and operating a hospital was untenable. The next best option was to find an operator with the money to buy the place and bring it up to the latest healthcare standards. My attempts to do that gobbled up an inordinate amount of personal time and energy. I couldn't easily delegate the task, because the negotiation had to be done privately to prevent even more pressure on the city, which in turn inflated the sales price. The more people yelled, the higher the asking price for the damaged buildings.

The mayor argued that the buildings were an eyesore and that we could and should simply condemn them. But to do so would risk litigation that might take years to resolve. Despite considerable public displeasure about my actions in the affair, I came to a purchase agreement. We reached it under great time pressure, because the mayor wanted to get the matter settled before he left office and I left town. As it was, the deal was none too good: it left us with no operator and inadequate funds to make the whole thing work.

Council member Cynthia Willard-Lewis, who became a state senator in 2010, representing New Orleans East, led the charge to get Methodist reopened. At first, the private operator seemed to take a reasonable view of the city's offer to purchase the site. The dilemma for me was that even though the area needed a hospital, the bed counts at local hospitals were actually falling— and operating costs rising—in post-Katrina New Orleans.

Several hospital providers were on the brink of bankruptcy. They didn't want another competing full hospital that would drain off healthy and insured people from their patient pool in the New Orleans East neighborhood. The mayor insisted on a thorough and detailed study to justify the purchase of Methodist. That looked like a runaround to the people in the East. They knew they needed a hospital, and they'd had one before Katrina.

We needed a strong case to get disaster funds to purchase the hospital, and to find an operator and financing. I worked on these issues night and day, negotiating behind closed doors to make a deal with the hospital ownership.

In the process, I became a target for abuse from people attending council meetings. The more those people screamed, the weaker our bargaining position became.

After long, hard negotiations, with Nagin and myself playing "good cop/ bad cop," we secured the rights to purchase Methodist at a price our budget could handle. I was relieved and very pleased: the hospital is the key to New Orleans East commercially. It was a tough slog, but we got it done. Subsequently, the incoming mayor got a better deal and hopefully the project will move, but even at this writing it is not complete.

Creating stronger neighborhood schools was also a critical element of our plan. A new Louisiana superintendent of education, Paul Pastorek, reached out to me early on. Paul is a small, athletic man with broad shoulders and lots of nervous energy. In the interests of developing a partnership between his agency and the city, we discussed sharing buildings, launching cooperative programs, and creating various funding schemes that would jump-start revitalization of the schools. Paul bought into our target area approach and decided that we should work together to design and build schools as backbones for helping neighborhoods recover. He needed to know which of them rated priority status and how they could be transformed.

As superintendent, Paul was saddled with too many school buildings in the wrong places, a product of racial segregation. Moreover, in New Orleans, he had to cope with a school district composed principally of semi-independent charter institutions with almost no operating capital.

We hit it off from the beginning. To effect a jump-start he wanted to install a new superintendent for the New Orleans area. After a national search, he selected one of my favorite schools people, Paul Vallas. I knew of Vallas's work from contacts in Chicago and Philadelphia.

Paul P. joined Paul V., creating a partnership for school reform aimed at matching curricula with the city's economic development priorities and development plan. We quickly decided on projects that would develop new curricula related to employment needs and opportunities in such fields as biotech, maritime, business/management, international management, creative arts, and community services. Our efforts led to the designation of disaster funds for some of those special high school initiatives as well as collaboration on the reuse of old, abandoned school buildings.

At the other end of the scale, we recommended that the Mahalia Jackson preschool program, in central city, receive disaster funds. Phyllis Landrieu, former chair of the New Orleans school district, led an effort to reestablish the program as a preschool, and it became the first project approved by the state.

Neighborhood recovery and housing are usually the province of a city's redevelopment agency. But in the case of NORA, a state-chartered entity with its own recovery plan, we had to negotiate the direction to take. After many conversations, we found common ground by awarding NORA $40 million for new projects and operations. We asked NORA to act like a city redevelopment agency within our target areas. The resulting contract commenced a novel process of restoring housing zones *around* the target areas. Small developers were invited to rebuild houses in selected neighborhoods like Pontchartrain Park, a historic African American suburb.

When we created ORDA, I discovered that we were knocking down twice as many houses as were being built. I therefore raised the bar on what could be torn down, and I got the mayor's support to stop razing houses in the target areas.

We set up a program to ensure more surgical house removals. Classic, traditional housing was preserved if it wasn't falling over. We worked with the Preservation Resource Center of New Orleans to purchase and rehabilitate as many homes of that type as possible. At first, it was difficult to obtain federal funds for housing preservation. My staff therefore reprogrammed the city's budget for low-income and moderate housing so it could support preservation initiatives. In addition, I asked the feds for a waiver to allow their funds to be used for that purpose.

We didn't get as far in that direction as I would have liked, but we did get a lot of preservation done. When I left my position, the Preservation Resource Center of New Orleans presented me with two books in recognition of the work I'd done: *New Orleans' Favorite Shotguns* and *New Orleans: Life in an Epic City*. "Preserving the past in New Orleans homes," I said at the book presentation, "is creating the city's distinctive future."

NEW ORLEANS IS ONE OF THE SADDEST RACE STORIES IN THE nation. The cumulative and historic race issues are enormous, and little has been done to change them.

New Orleans may be a glamorous place on its face. But beneath the glitter a devastating poverty festers that Katrina made all too public. The poverty rate in Louisiana is the nation's second worst. In New Orleans itself, 38 percent of all black kids live below the poverty line, and among fourth graders, only 44 and 26 percent read and do math at their grade performance, according to Phyllis Landrieu. As one former New Orleans public school principal and community leader said to me, "You don't need no readin' 'n' 'rithmetic to make a bed." The school dropout rate is higher than 50 percent, and the adult illiteracy rate is 33 percent.

African Americans make up more than a third of the families in the state, and nearly half the people in the poor category live in New Orleans. Of the 245 largest cities in the nation (populations over 100,000), it was the sixth poorest at the time of Katrina and eighth in 2009. More than one-fifth of the city's residents affected by the hurricane lived in poverty. Black incomes are less than half those of whites: the New Orleans Gini coefficient, the measure of income inequality between blacks and whites, is among the highest in the nation. New Orleans is ranked as one of the most violent cities on the planet, with the vast majority of the violence occurring in black communities. The chances of a black male going to prison in New Orleans are 20 times higher than going to college or university. And in Louisiana as a whole, most of the 37,000 men and women behind bars are black, and most are under forty years of age.

I walked regularly in my first neighborhood in Central City. One morning just after I arrived, I was strolling on the wide median strip where the trolleys ran. Post-storm, the area looked like a dust bowl. On this morning, I happened to come up behind two older white males who were walking their dogs and talking in very audible tones. They didn't acknowledge my presence. I listened as they discussed the additional guns and other armaments they planned to stock for the next hurricane.

"We weren't prepared this time," said one, loudly to ensure that I heard. "We shoot niggers on sight." They laughed.

I felt uncomfortable, so I moved off the trolley path to the sidewalk. As I did so, the other man said, also in a loud stage whisper, "Shit, man, you oughta *see* all the guns, grenades, and stuff we got in Mississippi. People there are prepared."

I stopped listening.

Later in the day, I said to the mayor, "Race relations are rough here."

He smiled and said, "You'll see."

The week I arrived in New Orleans, Tulane president Dr. Scott Cowen told the *Times-Picayune* in response to my appointment that if I couldn't solve the race problem, I couldn't succeed with a city recovery. When reporters asked me about Cowen's statement, I responded simply that I didn't yet know how central race relations would be to the recovery. I asked what other institutions were doing about the problem; after all, the race problems didn't come in with Katrina's waters.

No doubt I was viewed and hired as a potentially nonthreatening agent amid the racial strife. It might have been hoped that I could transcend racial lines or be accepted, as an outsider, as a neutral party. But as it turned out, both sides seemed to use my actions against me and sometimes even against their own aspirations. I found it hard to fathom why collaboration at some level didn't emerge and why, to the people I met and the press, the recovery seemed less important than the personalities involved.

In New Orleans, with its history of creoles and other mixed bloods, the racial-political dynamics are nuanced. The lighter you are and the straighter your hair, the higher you stand on the social and economic pecking orders.

The poorest residents have historically been the least likely to own an automobile, and the most likely to live in the wards most devastated by the hurricane and floods. The victims shown in dramatic photos were nearly all black—simply because many of the city's black residents didn't own cars, and so couldn't escape. Even worse, those who did own autos were stranded because they didn't have the money to buy gasoline when the storm hit—two days before welfare checks were due in the mail. By contrast, only 15 percent of whites lacked autos; even whites on welfare had networks of more affluent friends and relatives who were able to assist them in dealing with fuel and related emergencies so they could escape the coming disaster. One reporter said that when she interviewed middle-class refugees from the Gulf Coast, they criticized the government and the news media for giving too much attention and money to poor African Americans in New Orleans.

Race, income, and ownership play a large role in who gets what in New Orleans. Many blacks were renters and not owners. And they rented from the notoriously incompetent city housing authority. Even before the hurricane, the agency was trying to displace blacks from housing that it considered too near the city's favored quarters and to sell those properties to private developers for higher-income condos. That's one reason that the "green dot" plan for a privately led recovery was seen plausibly as a "racist plot."

New Orleans was and still is divided across "subracial" lines embodied in the spoils of the city's political structure. Middle-class blacks escaped from the poorest neighborhoods by establishing Pontchartrain Park and then New Orleans East. That partly explains why the city encompasses so many internal political jurisdictions: each racial caste holds its perch in the political system by maintaining control of a local jurisdiction.

In the aftermath of Katrina, race even affected the degree to which whites outside the South were willing to come to the aid of their fellow Americans. A controlled study carried out by the *Washington Post* concluded that "people were willing to give assistance to a White victim, on average, for about 12 months. But for an African American victim, the average duration was a month shorter, while the amount of aid was nearly the same, meaning that blacks would collect about $1,000 less than white victims." The *Post* later concluded that "Color is the key in New Orleans. This is even more so the case now that local blacks have seen firsthand how their fates are handled by the plantation aristocracy of New Orleans." Olshansky and Johnson add that in the case of New Orleans, "the biggest historic wrong was racial discrimination, not something that could be easily righted by rebuilding the city."

The data cited are a condemnation of a system. Tellingly, the only march against crime I witnessed in New Orleans came in the aftermath of a white woman's slaying. While I lived there, violent crime involving "black on black" drew condemnations but no public outrage. These data are bad enough; worse is that the victims are routinely blamed.

The 1927 New Orleans flood epitomized, tragically, this still-pervasive "plantation" attitude. Blacks were used as human sandbags and basically reenslaved by whites as the waters rose on the Mississippi. As the river subsided, black leadership reasserted itself in New Orleans. After the flood, Le-Roy Percy, the patrician flood commander, appeared at a large black church gathering in New Orleans, where he accused blacks of not being grateful to the white leadership after he had, as John Barry puts it in *Rising Tide*, "more than acquiesced when the Mississippi National Guard held black refugees in camps, forcing them to work on levees in conditions close to slavery," and destroying their homes to try to save the city from the floods.

The notion that blacks are responsible for their poverty and mistreatment is endemic among most whites in New Orleans. For example, the state felt it had to take over the financially starved and corrupt New Orleans parish school district run predominantly by a black-led school board with black administrators.

Similarly, the Housing Authority of New Orleans, the largest public housing agency in the nation, became unmanageable when its properties became de facto warehouses for large numbers of poorly educated, underskilled, and/or low-income blacks. The response was to tear down the housing, not to grapple with these underlying social problems—or the drug use, crime, and poverty accompanying them.

One can detect what could be called social distance, and not just income disparity. Blacks and whites share the same place in New Orleans, but they don't share the same destinies. Nor do groups within the African American community. Middle-class blacks live in almost exclusively middle-class black areas. Except for a few of the avant garde, the races don't socialize together. One of the planning commissioners I became friendly with referred to the occasional exception as "crossing the line."

Mardi Gras is still a segregated celebration. That is glaringly evident in the krewes. They sponsor Mardi Gras floats and function as social clubs in the off-season. And with few exceptions, they're deeply segregated. After I spoke before a "young leaders" group, a male member came up to me to tell me he had quit a krewe. A newcomer to New Orleans, he had worked hard to get into the sponsoring club. Finally, he received an invitation from a new friend to come to a krewe event, with entry into the club a distinct possibility, the kreweman assured. At his first meeting, the racial jokes began to flow thick and fast. The man couldn't and wouldn't participate in the joking, so he felt isolated. A few meetings later, he noticed a decidedly cool atmosphere toward him. He quit.

Blacks didn't have permission to march in Mardi Gras blackface parades until the 1970s. That means a good many of the festival's leaders who upheld such segregation are still there today. The civil rights, liberal adaptation is to allow blacks to march with their own floats and, at the conclusion of the parade, to rally at a segregated venue.

In my grandstand visit to the 2009 Mardi Gras, I witnessed the King of Rex (the white king) tethered to his wagon and unable to properly toast the black mayor. That kind of snub is not unusual. Mardi Gras ends with a public ceremony in which the black and white kings of the carnival meet on a barge in the Mississippi, coming from opposite sides of the river. The connotations are easy to see. Blacks, you keep your place, and we whites will keep ours.

I noted to the mayor on more than one occasion that the local newspaper of record had no black reporters working the city beat. This is astounding in a city that is 63 percent black and has several university programs in various media studies that attract large numbers of black students.

I also asked the mayor to explain how in 2007 there could be New Orleans social clubs (for example, the Boston Club) that he couldn't join because he's African American. The Boston Club played a key role in the way the white establishment dealt with the 1927 floods, when the even the white mayor of the city who was not in the elite club was left out of the decision making. Moreover, ideas expressed by the *Times-Picayune* originated largely with Boston Club members. The paper is still owned by a family that consorts with the club's white-only members privately, while saying little about this form of segregation publicly.

Informal social relations were segregated as well. One evening, a fire alarm rang at my house. My housemate set it off by putting the wrong code into my entry system for the front door. By the time the emergency responders left, it was late. I stood bewildered in my front yard. One of my white neighbors came out on her porch and asked if I needed help. I said no, but added, "I don't know a lot of people here." She responded that she assumed some of the black people in town would take care of me. As it turned out, my most adjacent African American neighbor did start looking after me.

My experience with race relations in New Orleans was no aberration. Elijah Anderson, a leading black social anthropologist, tells a story of a black and a white living across a back fence from each other. The white man enjoyed fishing. When he brought home more fish than he could use, he would call his black back-fence neighbor and offer him the surplus. But never in twenty years did the white man ask the black one to come through the gate in the fence. Anderson goes on to say, "you have to do what you have to do to deal with white people every day, but they are not to be trusted."

Sadly, some of my own staff expressed those views openly. In an off-the-record interview, I confessed my disenchantment with them to a *New York Times* reporter, who promptly reported it. The *Times-Picayune* expressed outrage in print.

I wondered what alternate universe the *Times-Picayune* lives in. All the post-Katrina ethnographies laid out this continuing saga of black versus white, in and out of city government. As Anderson observed in Birch and Wachter's book on Katrina, common wisdom among Southern blacks holds that if it had been white people stranded and seeking refuge, the government would have come to their aid. Nagin bluntly said in a California speech to a civil rights group: "Black people . . . are treated as if they do not belong to the body politic and are dispensable in a disaster. Anderson and others document how the two races coexist with each other, without trust on either side."

A few weeks after my experience with emergency services, on my Saturday walk with my friend Steve Bingler, we stopped at our usual corner coffee shop. I glanced at the morning headlines. One of the front-page stories concerned the city's changing racial mix. I bought a newspaper and took it to a table while Steve got the coffee. As I began reading the article, I became aware that a couple of white males nearby were discussing the same story—in relation to the larger white electorate. One pointed at the paper, poking the pages as he talked. "We got rid of Thomas," he said, referring to Oliver Thomas, former city council president and heir apparent to Mayor Nagin. "We can get the rest of 'em, too. 'Nig' Nagon [sic] has to go. We can win the council and get a real mayor. There's blood in the water; we can take this city back." Steve rejoined me, and we discussed the article for a few minutes.

As I walked the few hundred yards back to my house, another meeting came to mind, months earlier, when Thomas was still city council president. Thomas had burst into the mayor's office with no appointment, very agitated. I was just concluding a meeting with the mayor. Nagin is a big handsome man, about 6'2" and wide shouldered, with my skin coloring. Thomas was concerned that the mayor was featured as helpless in hostile articles and editorials in the *Times-Picayune*.

I started to leave the room. Thomas said, "Sit, Doc, this is about you, too, all of us. Ray, this ain't about you. They already got Jeff (referring to Representative William Jefferson, under indictment for graft and corruption). They're moving on some others on the school board. Somebody is talking. We barely held the job (mayor), we can't just hand it to them. They got unity. They gonna knock us off one at a time. You gotta get your act together for all of us."

At the end of a regular meeting with the mayor, I mentioned the "blood in the water" comment. He said to me, frowning, "You haven't seen anything yet." A few months later, as speculation increased as to who the mayoral candidates might be, I appeared on WBOK radio. On the air, I wouldn't discuss the array of candidates. But off the air, I mentioned the "blood in the water" comment. One of the hosts immediately replied that everyone knew "they" wanted their city back.

The municipal elections of 2010 seemed to give it to them. Mitch Landrieu, who is white, was elected mayor, and whites emerged with a 5-3 majority on the city council. After this outcome the black-owned *New Orleans Tribune* observed, "the causes and sources of black inequality have not been eliminated, nor have the disparities that negatively impact the quality of life of everyday black Orleanians."

As the president of Tulane observed when I was first appointed, I needed to focus on the right problem—race—and not just on reconstructing buildings. Race was far more important than building, because what Barry describes after the floods of 1927 might apply equally to the hurricane of 2005: "Out on the water there was unimaginable silence. As far as the eye could see was an expanse of brackish chocolate water. There was not the bark of a dog, the lowing of a cow, the neighing of a horse. Even the trees turned dingy, their trunks and leaves caked with dried mud. The silence was complete and suffocating" the will and spirit of the people.

13. A MEDIUM OFF MESSAGE

AS I BEGAN PACKING MY OFFICE FOR MY DEPARTURE FROM New Orleans in May 2009, I came across Marshall McLuhan's pioneering book on one of my shelves. His famous statement about the media being the message I found to be partially correct in New Orleans: there, during the recovery, it seemed that the media *made too many* messages.

In my time as recovery czar, I became an object of print news scorn but received generally good treatment from the major television networks in the city. My overall impression is that the mayor and I too often became scapegoats for a city that was devastated *before* Katrina, and that preferred to blame a slow recovery on Nagin, or my office, and to look for a quick fix in lieu of dealing with those underlying problems.

I may have deserved some of the print media criticism, or brought some of the scorn on myself. My job as I saw it involved getting a recovery done. That meant acting as something of a missionary for a total government overhaul. As one radio show host told me, I just didn't play the print media game. And I occasionally said things that were inappropriate.

Yet those were hardly legitimate reasons for the media to focus on me rather than on the recovery activities. When we made our recovery plan, news reports said it lacked sufficient funding. I explained that for a plan to be implemented, the planners had to *get* funds. Subsequent reports made it look as though I didn't know how to do that. When I did, I pointed out that it would take months to do the required architecture and engineering work before projects could begin. I went on to say there would be some cranes on the skyline by September. When asked what I meant, I looked at the questioner incredulously and explained that the phrase was a common metaphor for getting projects started, not a literal reference to cranes, pile drivers, or heavy equipment.

The day I made that comment, however, Mayor Nagin took me back to his office and said, "You shouldn't have said that. If they don't see a crane on every building in town, they will use it against you."

He couldn't have been more right. Well before my self-imposed September "deadline," cranes—as well as heavy lifts and pile drivers—appeared throughout downtown. With our GO Zone bonds, we funded commercial structures, most of them hotels and major facilities such as the city's first Nike store, the first major-chain book store, and the Louisiana Cancer Center, so close to City Hall that you could see the cranes rising. Yet they went unnoted by the print media. Tulane Avenue residential projects, supported with city and state funds, were also sporting cranes. I even distributed maps showing where they were located, and I sent photos of them that appeared on television—but not in print, where the columnists continued with their nonsense.

On my last day, when an AP reporter came to see me, I asked if she had seen the several cranes on the streets she would have had to have traveled to reach my office. She looked stunned. I also pointed out the cranes working on the Superdome. Nonetheless, she led her story with a comment about how few cranes were visible on the skyline!

Making up "gotcha news" became the main media game. A TV investiga-

Me with the Press.
Author's photograph

tive reporter, the only exception to my good treatment from television journalists, spent considerable time and money to find out what I'd done while engaged by the City of Oakland. He found a couple of journalism professors who weren't involved in the recovery, and got them to make comments on air. In addition, a disheveled Oakland city council member couldn't recall what I did, even though the filming for the program appeared to have been done in a building I'd helped to restore. Former mayor Elihu Harris later commented, "What would he know? He was just my driver. You were my leader." The council member who appeared on camera knew that, but chose to ignore it.

Harris strongly endorsed my role. So, apparently, did other key players in the Oakland recovery. I gave the TV reporter all their names, and some said they offered positive comments. But they didn't get return calls after his initial interviews. He managed not to find a single person who had been a participant in the fire or earthquake. I had run for mayor of Oakland in 1998, finishing a weak second to Jerry Brown, ex-governor of California, precisely *on* my record in these disaster recoveries. So the entire city was aware of my role in the fire and earthquakes. Yet to judge from the reporter's interviewing pattern, I was either a stranger or poorly regarded there. Later, Mayor Nagin asked me repeatedly if I had ever experienced a similar media problem. I couldn't recall a single instance.

Some months later, the same TV reporter interviewed me about the city's annual Community Development Block Grant funds. I brought along piles of records on the topic. He showed no interest in any of them.

But just before I gave the interview, one of my staff pulled me aside and said, "Do you know his wife works for the project we discussed earlier? You know, the Crescent/Riverfront proposal that was catching hell from the New Orleans East community because they think the money ought to go to the hospital in their community?" When I looked at him questioningly, he added: "That Riverfront project will never get exposed as a boondoggle for the wealthy river property owners on that television channel, Doc, no matter what they do."

I asked the reporter about this obvious conflict of commitment, if not interest. His reply: "My wife and I keep these things strictly separate."

After the interview, I relayed the TV reporter's comment to the staffer. I added, "This is the same guy who couldn't find the people in Oakland, like the vice mayor and others who had positive things to say about my work there. So I am sure he can't find his wife to talk her about the Riverfront, either."

City-owned public television became my tool for conveying images and other evidence of the recovery to ordinary people. I'd had a TV show associated with my campaign for mayor in Oakland, and I knew that the city public channel provided an underused communications resource. Websites are fine for reaching people you know or who are looking for you. Television provides an in-home communication that's random. Americans watch over 150 hours of television a month, and in New Orleans after the storm, residents spent much of that time glued to city public television to get updates on the recovery.

Few New Orleans people subscribe to daily newspapers or buy single copies of them, and even fewer, so far, regularly use blogs. Blogs are group reinforcing, in any case: writers talk to other writers like themselves. And most people in New Orleans who have computers don't use them to get the news.

On the city's channel one of my staff organized a series of shows that illustrated and documented the progress of the recovery. The series, called New Orleans on the Move, hit the mark. The aim was to show local residents how the city was working in this post-crisis situation and what we were doing in the recovery. Some of the segment titles:

1. Safety & Permits—how to get a residential permit, post-storm.
2. Affordable Housing—what new affordable housing is being built, and loan programs available for returning and new home buyers.
3. Library System—improvements to provide libraries with food and stationery so they could serve as community resource centers.
4. Riverfront Development—a program to build new commercial, residential, and park space along the Mississippi.
5. Regional Planning/Medical Center Complex— details about the pending new hospital complexes and their economic benefits to the city.
6. NORD (New Orleans Recreation Department)—a new program, and centers being built in the wake of the storm.
7. Economic Development—pending commercial projects the city will be stimulating.
8. Code Enforcement—dealing with blight and vacant properties.
9. Mahalia Jackson Performance Center—the rebirth of a performance-space icon.

Topics of our public service announcements included illegal dumping, abandoned swimming pools, the importance of moving FEMA trailers before hurricane season, requests to residents to remove harmful items form their properties or make sure these items were properly secured from children or vermin.

I found people to be far less cynical about me and the recovery than the press reports indicated. Moreover, our message was not misinterpreted by its intended audience. The message was working.

That was a valuable lesson about the media for me, and for other disaster recovery managers in the future: if you want to get your message out, use your own media outlets. These public service announcements and programs—as well as my website, blogs, and columns—are now my media presentations. Through them, I had some control over what I wanted to say, and could use it to build my own message and image.

14. LEVEES AND FEMA: THE REAL HAZARDS FOR NEW ORLEANS

IN ONE OF MY VERY FIRST FIELD NOTES IN NEW ORLEANS IN January 2007, I wrote, can the city fool Mother Nature? That question is still relevant, ominous, and unanswered. In some ways, it is a foundational question for the ongoing recovery. The levees render the city a cup with a sinking bottom. The city faces the mighty Mississippi on one side and a big lake on the other. Its unique geo-hazards must be confronted.

Every two weeks, usually on Friday, the New Orleans District of the Corps of Engineers brought a small army of military and civilian experts to discuss how they could make the city safer. Mayor Nagin controlled the flow of discussion. Although he grew a bit irritated with the Corps' voluminous Powerpoint slides, he asked good, often-unnerving questions about the speed and directions of potential hurricanes and their impacts.

The mayor's instincts were good. Not wanting to take chances, he ordered the evacuation of the city in September 2008 as Hurricane Gustav approached. His concern was not the Corps' levee plan but the potential for Gustav to sweep across the Mississippi from the east and destroy many of the city's inadequately protected areas. Protection was poor, at best, for Katrina, and now the Corps would be relying on an updated version of that program. Patching the levees is much like putting a new weld on broken steel structural supports. The welded area doesn't break, but the adjacent areas fail when new stress or forces are put on the adjacent fused components.

The mayor said, "We can't fight tomorrow's battles with the techniques that lost the last one." He is right.

The mitigation of future disasters depends on luck and science. If New Orleans is lucky, there won't be more Category 5 hurricanes, and seas will rise slowly and modestly. Realistically, however, the latest sea level models don't paint a rosy picture. The earth's oceans are warming fast. The oil spills of 2010 won't help matters, with habitat loss harming the landscape and increasing the potential damage from sea surges. And as sea surface temperatures rise, so do storm intensity and the resulting storm-surge force.

As the number of hurricanes increases, there is new evidence of sea and wind forces of magnitudes larger than those of Katrina. Where those storms will hit is of course unknown. We do know that Katrina breached the levees as only a Category 1 when it hit New Orleans. Professor Ivor van Heerden of Louisiana State University, the most knowledgeable of all Katrina hydrologists, shows clearly in his 2006 book *The Storm* that the levees fell with the storm at Category 1, well before the gales reached Category 5 status. According to van Heerden, the plan the Corps is embarking on will cost $30 billion, and will be a political solution that offers no new protection for New Orleans.

The Mississippi is rising higher with each flood. Data we put together from the national flood service at the University of Louisville indicate unacceptable future risk for much of the city. These data forecast severe and repetitive

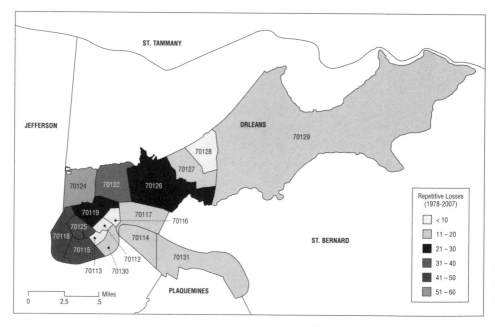

Repetitive and severe flood areas.

flooding from the Mississippi, rain, and tidal surges, so the known risks are complex. The city's geography restricts the practical options available under the levee strategy. If seas rise to only *half* the new projected levels, losses will be catastrophic in an extreme sea, lake, and wind event.

The most reasonable option is to live with more water. Let it run under and through the city. As van Heerden demands, "we must immediately move forward on two fronts: a major barrier and large-scale wetlands creation. No more Band Aids."

Van Heerden's idea is similar to the Dutch approach. They aren't protecting Amsterdam, which lies outside the flood areas. They're protecting farm and industrial areas. Moreover, Dutch investments in anti-flood technology are the only way to secure an entire nation of over 16 million with a GDP of $654.9 billion (in contrast to Louisiana's shrinking population of four million and the New Orleans metro area's population of just over 1.3 million). The Corps objectives are to improve levee protection to a 1 in 100 event level. That's what the agency has promised will be in place by 2011. It's better than what New Orleans had before Katrina, but much less than what is ideal for long-term planning. And it makes New Orleans more rigid and less able to absorb water as the seas rise with climate change. The Dutch, in contrast, are protecting against events of 1 in 10,000.

As Barry describes, the installation of levees has been a battleground since the 1850s, when they were first proposed. At that time, two great engineers waged a public war on how to control the great river. Andrew Atkinson Humphreys of the Corps of Engineers championed levees along the river, and, on the other side of the epic fight, James Buchanan Eads judged the levees to be useless and proposed that the solution was to sink piers below the surface to deepen the river but let it flow.

I think Eads had what is still the right idea. We should employ a flows strategy that allows more water to run through the city, by reusing the old canals and water paths that the original New Orleans was built around.

We should also explore the option of moving all or part of the Port of New Orleans to the Atchafalaya River Basin—or north toward Baton Rouge. The Native Americans encamped at Baton Rouge viewed the banks of the Mississippi there as a better and safer location than farther downstream near present-day New Orleans.

The notion of moving the city from the bend in the river goes back to another noted pre-Civil War engineer, Charles Ellet, who argued in 1851 that levees increased the danger of flooding. After studying all the means of taming the Mississippi, Ellet wrote, "I have pretty near come to the conclusion that instead of controlling these floods to maintain New Orleans, it would be a service to sweep away New Orleans with all its boarding houses, grog shops and music to boot." Ellet was being not petulant but realistic. He reasoned that the force of the river was greater than any manmade corset that could be put on it.

Change that drastic will require a program that gradually moves businesses and other property either north or east to areas less likely to flood regularly—and that also moves the Port of New Orleans to another location entirely on the Atchafalaya River. Such relocation will be cheaper in the long run. But it must be accompanied by a compensation scheme that recognizes current land values for all the movers, so that if they move voluntarily, they will get the same amount or even more, better-situated land, in the new area. Although the cost-benefit analysis is a tricky matter, the concept deserves consideration. If we fail to provide that, we're merely waiting out the inevitable next disaster.

My knowledge of these dangers was outweighed by the countervailing force set in motion by the political apparatus. I incorporated into the Target Area Plan the notion of a land swap. But to implement a swap would have required enormous collaboration among state bureaucracies, as well as cooperation from the Corps of Engineers. With help from the Corps, one of my staff developed a plan to move people to high ground and provide buyouts similar to those the agency had used in Kentucky and the Missouri Valley.

But one arm of the Corps was not in sync with the other. The builders of dikes didn't want any portion of the levee money diverted to such a scheme. Nonetheless, my staff, together with the University of New Orleans, developed very plausible albeit unrealized plans for moving homes away from danger.

My best possibility for the movement of people out of harm's way as recovery czar was my ill-fated blight-bond plan, which I hoped would provide enough money to induce people to swap blighted properties on high ground for those on low-lying land. The closest we came to that was the use of the second-mortgage scheme, tilted so that loans went first to properties in the higher-elevation target areas. Even though this was an indirect approach, the data showed that people were taking advantage of it.

The Road Home program that provided compensation or buyouts of Katrina flood-damaged homes put up the funding for these transactions. "Lowland" owners could buy property on higher ground, using a $60,000 "soft" mortgage that ORDA provided and that didn't have to be repaid if it was held for more than three years. This scheme worked. The data developed by Greg Rigamer, head of one of the city's best demographic and economic firms, showed a substantial movement of housing stock and businesses into the target areas, which, to be fair, are only marginally safer places in which to locate.

I've been criticized for not rebuilding the Ninth Ward, the most heavily damaged part of the city. My reasoning was simple: if you rebuild the Ninth, you're only asking for trouble, because it will wash away again in the next big storm.

We have a responsibility to future generations to build on solid ground, away from harm. The pending New Orleans City Master Plan and City Zoning Ordinance adopted in August 2010 has elements in it that can help set the direction by allowing water to move through the city as it once did, reducing the areas of severe flooding. Canals should be reopened to let the water flow through designated river outlets. Anyone visiting New Orleans is struck by the poor road conditions. Some streets have literally sunk below the curb lines, leaving large sinkholes all over the city. Offshore oil extraction is causing compaction of the Delta soil, a phenomenon whose negative impact is aggravated by the local practice of residences and businesses constantly pumping water out of their basements or from under storage areas of buildings.

The New Orleans storm defenses were designed in the 1960s to withstand one storm per century, landing 75 miles from the city. The defenses failed to meet even those modest expectations. Category 5 protections come at a cost of $30 billion, with no guarantee that they will work. The likelihood of a C5 hurricane is increasing, at the same time that the vulnerability of the land itself is increasing because of the levees' brittle, stationary state. In the event of a real C5 storm that hits the city directly, as Virginia Burkett points out, such a storm in New Orleans "would place [a street intersection in the center of the city] at least 9 meters below storm-surge level." James Hansen, director of the NASA Goddard Institute of Space Studies, describes the increasing dangers of sea rise for New Orleans: "A meter of sea level rise would be enough to turn New Orleans into the new Big Easy Reef."

The bottom line, according to Judith Curry, chair of the School of Earth and Atmospheric Sciences at Georgia Tech, should be daunting to all residents and lovers of New Orleans: "A hundred years from now, there's no way there's going to be a city here. . . . This is just the way geology and climate work."

Robert Giegengack and Greg Foster closed their presentation on the futility of the current approach by paraphrasing the Rev. Jesse Jackson: "You can fight city hall [as New Orleanians like to do] if you choose, but you might lose. You can fight gravity if you choose, but you're sure to lose.

Work done by local architects is similar to the work of Anuradha Mathur and Dilip da Cunha, experts who reviewed the Katrina disaster, who point out, in Birch and Wachter, *Rebuilding Urban Places*, "This may be a useful moment to seed an appreciation of a world of flow . . . [for the Mississippi River] . . . by seeding new infrastructure that . . . respond to a fluid, perhaps living terrain rather than assume the strength and security of enclosures."

There are signs that New Orleans and other cities recognize the dangers and the need to alleviate them. To restore the old Mississippi flows, New Orleans is building the Lafitte Greenway, which reconnects nine neighborhoods with a grassy spine that will allow water to move freely. Segments of Grand Forks, North Dakota, and several other cities along the banks of the Mississippi—including, in Louisiana, from Isle de Jean Charles to Houma—were moved to provide for greater safety for the larger communities downstream or upstream. As argued above, consideration must be given to moving some parts of New Orleans as well.

What about FEMA?

I testified before Congress on several occasions, saying that we can and should fix that agency to equip it to deal effectively with catastrophes like Katrina. In my view, FEMA should be part of the Department of Homeland Security. But the rebuilding of devastated communities, rural or urban, requires more than the current rules and roles provided for FEMA under the Stafford Disaster Relief and Emergency Assistance Act.

As officials in New Orleans and now other cities are learning, it takes a range of agencies to restore the commercial life—as well as the health, security, and vitality—of a severely damaged city: for example, Health and Human Services, together with Justice, for community health and physical and social security; Housing and Urban Development for housing; the Environmental Protection Agency for water and sewers; and the Small Business Administration and Commerce for businesses small or large. The Stafford Act and FEMA are inherently too limited to play all those roles effectively.

President Obama demonstrated that he recognizes those limitations when he required that all his Cabinet offices develop better strategies to aid communities in the aftermath of a disaster. I therefore used my congressional testimony to suggest steps that might stimulate a productive discussion on the entire subject. The steps:

1. *Create a new national disaster-recovery organization to coordinate federal agency activity.* Although FEMA has improved its post-disaster capacities, its major mission emergency evacuation and response, the government needs a new coordinating entity that has the capacity to work with all federal agencies to establish and maintain a reliable federal response—a one-stop shop. No community, no matter how large, is in a position to figure out how to access the bewildering array of federal programs. The single, coordinating office should be located in the White House, and should have senior liaison personnel in all Cabinet-level departments and other major agencies.

2. *Establish a new federal disaster-recovery office in each region of the country* that would work under the new national coordinating agency, with the purpose of marshaling regional-level recovery resources, such as academic staff, major consulting organizations, and regional transportation. Those and other entities can offer expertise to cities as they begin the process of planning, organizing, and staffing to rebuild. This is important because few communities can afford such expertise beyond first responders and emergency teams. The regional teams would assist policymakers in assessing the damage and the options for repairing it.

3. *Establish a new National Recovery Fund.* Attempts to jury-rig community block grants for disasters have never been satisfactory. A single disaster fund, appropriated by Congress and administered by the coordinating agency or the Treasury Department, would be a far better approach. Since disaster relief is an off-budget item, that would require fiscal analysis to determine the size and use of the fund.

4. *Require states and localities to set aside their own disaster funding.* Many states have started and stopped so-called rainy day funds. It's time to rethink the need for a mandated percentage—2 or 3 percent—of each state and local governmental agency's funds to be placed in a "disaster account." That can be incentivized in several ways, including the provision of increased post-disaster assistance to communities that have already taken the precaution of establishing funds for their own protection.

5. *Build for the future, don't recreate the past.* Current FEMA formulas are based on rebuilding existing structures, which is seldom wise. A new approach would be to fund a recovery plan that takes into account not only a calculation of damage but also a broader assess-

ment of community needs for the future. The federal government would monitor such rebuilding to assure that it is consistent with the plan, but would not require the current building-by-building approach to determine funding. Once a plan and budget were in place, recovery would start without the present approach of getting money only after you've incurred the debts.

As the Stafford Act has been debated, we need a fresh view of where we are headed and a realistic understanding that the best preparation for dealing with future disasters involves twin initiatives: to plan *for them*; and then to rebuild to *avoid others*.

PART IV

Assessing the Recovery

15. CHANCE TO ASSESS THE RECOVERY

IN LATE NOVEMBER 2008, AS MY APPOINTMENT AND THE second term were coming to an end, Mayor Nagin and I met over lunch to take the next steps and begin changing the city's message from "recovery" to "normalcy." Continuous stories of struggle at some point wear out. There was talk in Congress of Katrina fatigue.

I discussed options with the mayor. We agreed that the recovery phase for the city needed to move on. At a budget hearing for 2009, the mayor and I put in place a new organizational approach that featured an office of community development. For me, that felt like coming full circle: community development is the idea to which I'd devoted my career.

After almost two years as executive director of ORDA, I was exhausted. My professional challenges and my tenure as recovery czar needed to be framed so that I could tell my story. I wanted to let my colleagues and others know what I'd done, and to take stock of the recovery myself. In addition, I felt the need to escape the pressure cooker of post-Katrina New Orleans politics, and to bounce my ideas off an intelligent, dispassionate audience.

The opportunity came in early 2009, when I was invited to Harvard to talk about New Orleans's recovery. I couldn't go until May, just prior to my departure from my post. I would be addressing students and faculty at the university's well-known Kennedy School of Government. During my first year in New Orleans, I had visited Harvard to present the recovery from the inside and to correct some of the misinformation and perceptions about it that were floating around the country. At that time, my work was just beginning, and I was hoping for good press and help with my work from Harvard colleagues

Now, I was looking back at the experience, curious to hear what others had to say—and ask—about it.

Duce and I had left for the airport late, and were soon racing down the same streets that I'd first come to know two years earlier. But this time they were alive. The trolley was rolling down the St. Charles Avenue median strip, with its green grass on each side. People were smiling and talking animatedly, as New Orleans folk do, with their hands moving as fast as their lips. The sky was not gray, as on my first day in January 2007, but a beautiful blue.

Duce was a master of reckless yet purposeful driving. He whipped around the dense commuter traffic—notably denser than when I had arrived in 2007—rode the shoulder of the road reserved for disabled cars, and honked at anything in the way. When we almost ran up the rear of a sheriff's vehicle from another parish, the deputy cleared a path for us, his sirens blaring, too. I worried about leaving New Orleans in a casket.

This time, however, speed didn't kill; it paid off. Bolting into the airport with five minutes to spare before my gate closed, I hit the security checkpoint at a full sprint. A TSA man on duty spotted me and waved me past the crowd.

"C'mon, Doc," he called. "We know who you are. Go get us some more money." I smiled, electing not to admit that I was going in search of intellectual approval rather than funding.

Now, on the plane to Cambridge, I took out my ballpoint pen, opened my notebook, and collected my jangled thoughts, based on the challenges I'd listed that first evening in New Orleans. It now seemed so long ago.

I outlined my entire experience as czar of the city's ungainly, halting, and confused reconstruction job—the high points, the many low points, the challenges, the lessons, the good, the bad, the ugly. If the Harvard community wanted to know what this czar business was like in New Orleans, how frustrating and in the end difficult it turned out to be, I would tell them, straight out. . . .

My Harvard appearance covered two days. The morning after the harrowing departure from New Orleans, I left my hotel and made the short walk to the Littauer Building, where most of the Kennedy School classrooms and offices are located. This is my favorite academic building in the world. When I was at the University of Southern California as dean of urban planning in 1995–2000, I used the Littauer Building as my model for a new academic structure to house USC's urban planning and public policy programs. At Littauer, students sit on steps and in little bullpens on the landings, talking and studying together. I like that. I felt as comfortable there as in an old shoe.

On the third floor, I was met by several members of the group that would join me in putting together the Harvard JFK case study. Introductions were perfunctory; I knew a few of these people, so we didn't dwell on formalities. There were three men and two women: a middle-aged fellow called D, athletic looking but overall more like an accountant than a professor, the leader of the school's crisis-management program; Arn, a fellow in his fifties; a guy on the phone named Doug, who seemed polite and turned out to say little; a female academic from my home area of Berkeley; and another woman professor, J. In all, the assembled group appeared to be comfortable in the Harvard surroundings.

Sitting down at the head of a light-colored oak table, I grinned and said, "This isn't the State Department exam room." D, the leader of the team, didn't get the joke. So I added, "The room arrangement, the table, and the looks on your faces bring back some old memories." D, a grad-school study in polo shirt and Dockers, relaxed and smiled. "Tell the New Orleans story the way you feel comfortable telling it," he said.

"Okay," I replied. "But interrupt me when I'm not being clear or you want more elaboration. I don't want to give you a blow-by-blow treatment."

Doug, the professor who'd been on the phone, said, "I have a question about Mayor Nagin. He was originally elected with a large majority, so he had considerable support from the community, right?"

The mayor enjoyed a strong support in his first term, I am told, from a broad cross section of blacks and progressive whites. This was not true for his reelection. His base was almost entirely whites who didn't like his white opponent and blacks voting for the black against a white candidate. It was a different and fickle constituency. So this issue of political distrust and hostility toward the mayor forms an important part of the background of my experience story.

I looked around. D was poised to write notes. Arn was stroking his chin. The Berkeley professor looked a bit bewildered.

D: How did you get started doing this job? For instance, who did you hire to help you?

In the first wave, I hired a staff of five through the city budget, and a total of 17. I brought aboard Jessie Smallwood, an old colleague from my antipoverty days in California. She was close to people at the Ford Foundation. She worked with me to develop our grant proposal to help fund recovery planning and staffing. I had good connections at Ford, too. In the first funding, Bill Gates's foundation joined Ford to provide an expanded staff for two years.

Arn: Gates?

Yes, the foundation's officials said they wanted to do something. So I hired a bunch of people at first with no budget at all until the foundation funds arrived. We needed, for example, a deputy director for day-to-day recovery operations. We also required help—a resource position for raising more foundation and government money. We needed a person to coordinate our neighborhood projects; a person with environmental credentials for all the environmental issues associated with the recovery, and a staff person to examine local, state, and national policies that we might be able to use to get more recovery funds for New Orleans.

I organized my own staff with the youngest qualified people I could find on the city's payroll; in case there were any city layoffs, I didn't want the young people to suffer.

Berkeley professor: So you had more staff than you planned for originally.

Yes, and we could not have developed the recovery plan without more, because I needed an intimate knowledge of the city's communities—along with the commitment and energy these people brought. They went into every neighborhood in the area we chose to focus the recovery on and conducted house-by-house assessments.

Berkeley professor: What did you do next?

We took the next two months to create our recovery plan. We dubbed it the Target Area Plan, because we needed to see the city though these small "target areas" of two to four square blocks as windows on the recovery.

Let me turn to what was for me the big issue: the economy. New Orleans is a great tourism-based economy. But tourism makes a notoriously insecure base, because it is affected by weather—especially disasters like Katrina—as well as sickness like swine flu and changes in oil prices or travel fads. And tourism is notorious for not generating a lot of good-paying jobs.

So we forged a strategy to rebuild the economy, not just the structures. That dovetails with one of your earlier questions about New Orleans politics. When we came up with this strategy, the mayor was supportive. Although the city council members nodded their heads in agreement, they didn't seem to understand what we wanted to do. However, they knew we needed a different economic direction, so they felt they should say okay to help get the recovery underway.

D: Did everybody go along with this approach?

Well, no. Cynthia Willard-Lewis, the most outspoken of the council members, said that the bulk of the money should go to the heavily devastated areas. I responded that most of the money would go to distressed areas, but pointed out that we had to put money into projects that would make a big difference in the economy so the city would have a future.

Federal funds can go to public infrastructure like street and city buildings. But in the Ninth Ward and New Orleans East, the biggest issues were individual houses, not public works. In addition, with the city's housing starting to deteriorate, the Ninth Ward and some places in the East didn't have a lot of people coming back to live in them. So we were facing a Catch 22: if we repaired homes and people didn't return, we would be creating a new problem of unused and potentially vandalized housing.

Professor J: How did the state and the feds respond?

Four months after I took over, we received preliminary approval from the Louisiana Recovery Authority for the $417 million; that's when I said that by September there would be cranes in the sky—meaning recovery projects underway. Projects did start in September, but we had not counted on several things. One was that the state viewed the $417 million from the federal government in community block funds as state, not New Orleans funds. In my earlier experiences with community development, block grants went directly to the city, once its budget had been approved. But in this case the state preempted our grants by reviewing every project, thus increasing the time spent in processing and slowing down everything.

D: This review, was it hostile or reasonably friendly?

In Governor Blanco's administration, parts of the state bureaucracy, like the audit department, were hostile. The administration seemed to assume that New Orleans was going to steal the money and that the city's officials were only there to take the money, not to get anything worthwhile done. They knew that our city council president was under indictment.

Professor J: Weren't several members of the school board also under indictment at the time? So you're saying that the idea of local public officials having the opportunity to decide how the money was spent in New Orleans sounded either foolish or just outrageous.

I nodded yes.

D: The city bureaucracy, were they helpful?

They couldn't be helpful. The City of New Orleans bureaucracy was still designed to deal with one case at a time. There was a massive refusal to accommodate what I call batch process. So when you approached them with eight or ten buildings to do, they said, "No, we don't do it that way." They took a de novo approach to every contract involving any agency we were going to give money to—even though the contracts looked exactly alike except that the name was changed. In short, getting the money and getting going was not easy.

Arn: Given the politics, the learning curve, all the distrust, and the historic record of corruption, you must have been worried about investing your own reputation.

Yes, but after the first full year I had crafted a totally new organization within the public bureaucracy called the Office of Recovery Development Administration, or ORDA as we called it. When I arrived, the intention was that my role would be to develop plans for the recovery and guide the line agencies in their implementation. I had no line authority, even though my office was called the Office of Recovery Management. Management in this respect meant managing plans and not staff or budgets of the line agencies like Capital Projects for buildings, Public Works for streets, Park and Recreation for parks and civic services.

As it turned out, the chief development officer and head of the line agency in charge of the mayor's office of economic development and housing, Donna Addkison, resigned under pressure from the mayor. Initially, I wanted to find a sympathetic replacement who would carry out the building of a new VA hospital and other large-scale development projects. But after a few weeks I was convinced that I needed a line agency to have equal footing with other bureaucrats in City Hall. No one respected an advisory role like the one I had in Oakland.

So, I took on the job of planning the recovery, advising the agencies, and running the economic development portfolio, which included key links such as city planning and permits as well as overall economic development and housing programs. With this organization, I suddenly had the opportunity to implement the Target Area housing initiatives, community planning projects like neighborhood services programs, and almost $60 million in HUD Community Block Grant funds that had not been spent because of the three years of not having projects while the city recovered. I therefore had the seed money to start neighborhood and housing recovery projects, and the leverage with this money and planning and permits to make NORA, the redevelopment agency, come to me for housing funds and community development dollars.

I also had complete control of the economic development program to guide the VA-LSU project I just described.

Arn: Were there some nervous nights when you'd lie awake?

Well, FEMA kept me awake. The top brass at FEMA were always polite and generous. But then, as you went down the line, people got out the pencil sharpeners.

But ORDA gave me no major problems. All in all, ORDA was a successful operation. We moved from 17 people to over 200 with the budget that could shape the recovery and staff who were able to implement many of the Target Area projects using the portfolios they already had.

Some of the mayor's key staff were hostile to this larger bureaucracy, because they saw in it the power I could exercise on my own. But the mayor himself was very supportive. By the time I signaled my departure, we were able to reshape the city administration into an ongoing operation based on the priorities set through ORDA. Our ORDA team was among the most respected in City Hall.

At that point, I checked the time and told the group, "I'm afraid that's it. I need to get ready to give my talk to students and the public."

I walked down a short hallway to a small, horseshoe-shaped auditorium. It was a pleasant place. The back of the room faced the street, so you could look out onto the courtyard.

There was one person in the room, my thirty-four-year-old daughter Pieta, a Harvard student. She came to me. She was sitting in the front row reading a magazine. When I said, "Well, you see I can draw a crowd," she started giggling. But people drifted in, and after about ten minutes the room was nearly full: young men wearing loafers and scraggy beards and frizzled long hair; a multiracial and multinational-looking group of women, wearing thong sandals and serious looks. A large man with a laptop and a big tape recorder was setting up, so he could record my every word. "That," I whispered to my daughter, "is the *Times-Picayune* 'truth squad.'"

At the end of my talk, I held up my hands. "It's time for me to go," I said. "Thanks for having me." The audience applauded warmly.

Pieta came up to the platform. She had a pleasant surprise for me, light years from what I'd been talking about. "Dad," she said, "great talk! Evan and I are getting married. Naturally, we want you to be at the wedding! I hope you can get some rest now." She grinned. "We need you."

I LEFT NEW ORLEANS AT THE END OF MAY 2009, WITH A GREAT send-off party given by Mayor Nagin and attended by about 150 guests. I received many accolades: for example, the proverbial "key to the city" and the designation of my date of departure as Edward J. Blakely Day. The city council were unanimously generous in their praise of my service.

At an event organized by my staff, I read from one of the many letters I'd received from returned residents, thanking me and urging me to "stay and finish the job." I did the media rounds and radio talk shows.

Everyone in the electronic media, and even many in print, seemed grateful that I had stayed as long as I did.

I left New Orleans when I could and should have left. The template for recovery was in place. I had recruited a successor along with a total new city organization approach to postrecovery managing. I put in motion the development of a city master plan that incorporated all the recovery goals and locations as well as the VA Hospital land purchases for a multibillion-dollar investment with thousands of new good paying jobs. I signed off on hundreds of projects that when approved would put cranes on the skyline for the next two or three years with more than half of all the streets in the city repaved, many with streetscaping, combined with a host of environmental programs designed to prevent or mitigate storm and flood damages across the city.

I had one last duty to perform, unofficially, as recovery czar: I was to accompany Mayor Nagin to China for a two-day visit. He would be going from there to Australia, where he'd been invited by my new academic unit—the

United States Studies Centre at the University of Sydney—to make a presentation on Katrina. The date for the visit was set before I decided to leave the city, but it was propitious for me. Nagin could see me in action on my home turf—in a sense, take me back home. I considered that a good omen.

A week after I returned home to Sydney, I boarded a plane for Shanghai. No longer an employee of the city, I was going to China at my own expense and as the mayor's colleague. One of our senior economic development specialists, Ernest Gethers, traveled with us.

I had made contacts earlier in the year, in Dubai, with officials of a Chinese sovereign wealth fund (a government entity to buy assets overseas). They described their particular fund as composed of all the U.S. dollars and foreign currency reserves they held and wanted to invest in real estate and real assets, not in more U.S. bonds and debt.

The officials were therefore interested in New Orleans partly, too, to help me out, since I had worked with them for many years on development in China. They expressed strong interest in helping the Methodist Hospital cover the gap between government funding and the total cost of rebuilding the facility.

I wanted to see that project through. The mayor had negotiated a good deal to secure the site; I felt responsible to find the money to make sure the plan became a reality.

In Shanghai, familiar territory, I took the bullet train into the city. The mayor's staff had arranged rooms for the group at a central hotel. I took a room there, too, to be close to his team. I arrived a half day before they did, and set up dinner with an Oakland Chinese American colleague who had strong Shanghai contacts. My Chinese American friends knew the group with the money better than I did, and in a business transaction in that country, it is always best to have at your side someone you know who has a Chinese background.

The Chinese Americans had come to New Orleans three or four times. They knew the city's needs, and they wanted to secure some kind of agreement involving China. They felt that if they could generate Chinese interest in New Orleans, money would be no object. After all, Chinese firms were reaching out across the world to make deals with all their newfound U.S. dollars.

My Chinese American friends and I had a quiet meal with several key Shanghai businessmen and -women. I knew the professor from the local Chinese Planning Institute. He acted as intermediary for the Chinese sovereign funds in any mainland Chinese investment outside the country. He runs a university-based consulting firm that works with Chinese interested in using their country's sovereign funds for international construction. Such firms, part of all Chinese deals, are designed to ensure a transfer of technology, not just cash, when foreign firms do business in China or outside the country.

When I asked how serious the Shanghai development group was regarding this New Orleans opportunity, I received strong assurances from the professor that a deal could be brokered involving the Chinese investment firm co-venturing with a New Orleans-based construction organization with the resources to make the deal work.

Sticking points remained. The Chinese firm needed a New Orleans partner, and an operator would have to be found. Even with a partner and an operator, local laws would require that the venture be put out for competitive bidding. The Chinese didn't understand that at all, and we couldn't get the point across to them. Their government had the power simply to award the contract, so why didn't ours? Furthermore, nobody in China had a certificate to work in the United States, and that, too, would be necessary.

The professor explained that the Chinese sovereign fund would like to build the hospital since they had considerable construction expertise. He showed me a list, with photos, of office buildings and apartment complexes the Chinese had built all over Asia and Africa. He said, "As you know, no one can build as fast as we can." The professor took me over to a big bay window in the restaurant, pointed to a massive 50- to 70-story structure, and said, "That building was not here when you came here in 2005." He talked more about the high quality of Chinese construction. Finally, after tea late in the evening, we adjourned.

I got up early the next day to rendezvous for breakfast with the mayor, his wife, a security person, and the New Orleans development team. We caught a bus to Wuxi, a mid-sized city a little over an hour from Shanghai on the Yangtze River. Our schedule included visiting a factory that made home building products. The firm expressed interest in opening a factory in New Orleans to capture a portion of the building-services market there. The products in question are simple to manufacture: the equipment isn't complicated to operate, and the potential for hiring local staff made it ideal for New Orleans. En route, the mayor and I discussed alternative locations for the factory. We had not discussed the project in detail, as we usually did on economic development issues, before we were both in China, because our employment was slow to return and we needed quick wins, we looked at the employment and overall economic potentials. It seemed like a good deal.

At the factory, we received the usual ultra-polite reception. English-language speakers were scant, but a Powerpoint presentation offered background on the firm along with all the requirements for inputs. We all left impressed.

As a visiting mayor, Nagin called on the local government leadership. Then we left for Shanghai. He needed to be there to address participants in a potential "investor-residency program." It awards visas that can lead to permanent residency for foreign nationals who invest more than a half-million job-producing dollars in the United States. The team that runs the program in China for the New Orleans region set up meetings at which the mayor could give presentations to participants.

Back at my hotel, I was making some notes when the phone rang, with a call bearing a big and unwelcome surprise. On the line was the mayor's international relations person, Lisa Ponce de Leon. Lisa asked me to come to the mayor's suite as soon as possible. When I replied, "Okay, but what's up?" she said only, "Please come now."

I arrived at the mayor's suite to find him in casual clothes pacing around the room. A Chinese official was present, along with several senior hotel staff. Lisa informed me that Mayor and Mrs. Nagin had been seated near a pair of H1N1 flu carriers on the plane from the United States. Initially, I felt no alarm. I had heard about quarantines for school kids and a few people from Mexico. I said, "The mayor is here on official business and should not be subject to this procedure. Surely a simple physical check will be sufficient for a public official."

Then I learned additional details: two passengers, a French couple, had tested positive for H1N1 when they got off the plane, and the incident had drawn the attention of senior Chinese health officials. A group of health officials were waiting downstairs in a conference room. Lisa kept addressing me as "Dr. Blakely." Picking up on her implication, I asked a few questions that a physician might ask, and went downstairs to meet the public health team.

I needed to get my Chinese American colleagues to the hotel as soon as possible. They could assist me with translations as well as make high-level contacts. My head was spinning. At the meeting, I tried to make my greetings in feeble Chinese and establish my position with the health officials. It quickly became clear, however, that this problem exceeded the rank and authority of the health officers in the room.

We had an international diplomatic incident on our hands.

I exchanged a few words with four or five of the Chinese officials. They looked and acted serious. It was already clear that the mayor could not fulfill the rest of his scheduled obligations. Lisa started making a new schedule, in case he was quarantined. Sooner or later—probably sooner—this incident might be international news.

Our New Orleans team huddled to consider the options. Could we get the mayor on a return flight to the United States? If we did, the Chinese could wash their hands of the affair. That solution didn't appeal to me. The mayor had a full schedule in Sydney, at "my" institution, including a speech at a major conference. We had arranged a "City Talk," one of Sydney's most prestigious events, in a large auditorium in the center of town. City Talks are big and open to the public, sponsored and hosted by the mayor of Sydney. In this instance, Mayor Clover Moore planned to exchange ideas with her New Orleans counterpart on the subject of sustainable city building.

Nagin's travel team went over every possibility. We worked on getting the U.S. embassy to take charge of the problems or get the Australians to intervene. The mayor, his wife, and the security staffer were isolated from the rest of us on the upper floors of the hotel. I expressed the hope that the Chinese authorities would respect the mayor's stature and simply let him go after additional health checks. That, the authorities replied, would not be possible.

I scrambled back to the conference room, where the Chinese officials were camping out. A more senior official now headed their public health team. She expressed sympathy for the mayor's case. I suggested intense medical exams, perhaps by the U.S. consulate in Shanghai or with its support. Although she seemed to see the value of that approach, she let me know that normal procedures involved at least five days of quarantine. I almost fell off my chair: if that rule were enforced, there would be no Sydney trip.

At that point, with my mobile phone out of juice, I borrowed one from a Chinese official and made calls to my Sydney and Washington contacts. I also called the professor I had dined with the night before. All expressed surprise that matters had taken this course.

Contacts are built up over years of world travel, and they make a difference. My mobile contains only a small portion of my thousands of contacts, which I carry with me in a large folio and use regularly. That list includes a lot of very senior retirees who can still make things happen in their old places of work.

I had started calling contacts when the hotel staff informed me that the mayor would be transferred to a quarantine site. We didn't know and couldn't find out the site's location. It was a state secret. The mayor, his wife, and the security officer were taken out of the building and placed in an ambulance under guard. I felt sick.

My contacts started returning my calls. They told me what I already knew: the mayor and his wife were infected Americans and had to be quarantined. The mood was growing increasingly pessimistic. I met with my Chinese American counterparts, and we set up a plan. I would call my colleagues in the United States and Australia to request that those countries intervene. Lisa would work with the U.S. consulate staff in Shanghai. We knew that the only thing we could do or hope to do was to get the mayor out of China—to the United States or Australia. I had some reservations about the latter, because few countries take disease, germs, or any bugs more seriously than does Australia.

But when I reached staff at the Department of Foreign Affairs in Canberra, they expressed sympathy. I convinced them that the mayor and his wife were healthy and not risks for the transmission of disease in Australia. I offered to add a precautionary step: a physical exam, if we could get the Nagins to a place that would administer one.

As I worked the phones, I faced another issue. Someone needed to represent Mayor Nagin if he couldn't make the meetings for the potential Chinese investors in New Orleans who were waiting to talk to him about immigrating to the U.S. on special recovery jobs visas. The U.S. immigration team wanted me to replace the mayor for this talk. Given my exposure and name recognition in China, they felt they could "sell" me to their country's immigration people if the latter proved difficult. So we proceeded with that plan.

At that point, getting out of Shanghai became important to me. I wanted to be in Sydney in case the mayor was late arriving. Meanwhile, I had business to attend to where I was. I represented the mayor to the first group of would-be Chinese-New Orleans investor-residents. Although distracted, I completed that task and then got on the phone to get a flight. (It occurred to me that these zealous heath officials might ask if I myself had been in close contact with the mayor and his wife, who were now in quarantine.)

I found that I could exchange my ticket for a flight the following day—after meeting with the potential Chinese hospital-development team. That session proved disappointing. The Chinese investor group were very haughty and only wanted to build a hospital on their terms. After our unproductive meeting, I went to the airlines ticket center and got a ticket endorsed to leave in a few hours.

On the flight to Sydney, I started making alternative arrangements in case the mayor *didn't* arrive. I kept in touch via Blackberry and telephone about what we were doing as long as I could in the lounge and on the plane. My spirits were dropping, but his remained high. If he could get out of China, he would come to Sydney as planned.

Buoyed by the mayor's enthusiasm, I again worked my contacts in China, the United States, and Australia to try to spring him from quarantine. Suddenly, the situation loosened up. I'm not sure how, but the mayor secured a release date. I called Qantas. The agent there assured me that if he got to the airport he would be able to board the next flight to Sydney. The U.S. Studies Centre team started putting things in place. Interviews were reorganized, and talks slightly altered in time and format.

The morning of Mayor Nagin's arrival, I was back where I started. I was wearing an official badge, courtesy of the Australian Department of Foreign Affairs, as an escort for a mayor and his party. I was traveling back through forty years of memories, recalling the many times I'd worn such a badge as a U.S. Foreign Service officer in the 1970s, walking down back hallways to greet a dignitary. I felt at home.

The visit went well. The mayor presented the rationale for, and challenges of, rebuilding a *better* city, not just restoring it. He described the difficulties of dealing with the U.S. federal administration and how often he had to appeal to Congress to get what he needed. Nagin impressed people throughout the city, and his comments drew strongly positive comments from the national media. He took Sydney like a storm.

The head of the U.S. Studies Centre, my colleague, told me emphatically, "He's a real prince."

I replied, "You just don't know. He's a great man."

After a day of seeing Sydney, including a visit to the world-famous opera house, the mayor joined me at my home and beach club. We met for the final time at his hotel.

We parted as we started—good friends and mutual admirers.

As I strolled from the hotel toward the harbor, I thought, "Here we are, Ray Nagin and I, both headed for uncertain futures. He won't be mayor much longer. And what will I do next?"

My Blackberry bleeped. My friends wanted to know if I could join them for tennis in the morning. I said yes and put the Blackberry back in its holster. I asked the driver to take me home by way of the spectacular Sydney Harbour Bridge rather than by the alternate route, a tunnel.

My Blackberry bleeped again. I asked the driver to take the next right turn. "Nice day for baseball," I mused aloud, not thinking I was in Australia, where baseball is not a big sport. The driver turned to me and asked, in heavily accented English, if I had learned to play baseball in America. "Yes, of course," I replied.

"Sir," he said, "you are having just slight American accent. You are not from America. Maybe you are from my country, sir."

"I'm American," I responded.

"What is your work, sir?"

"Well, I. . . ." My Blackberry bleeped. Two text messages had arrived. The first one said:

> You are the winner of the 2009 Chatterjee award from the Collegiate School of Planning for public and community service for your work in New Orleans and previous service to the profession
> —Charlie [Charles Connerly]

The second one read simply:

> Can you come back to Pudong?
> Your friend, the Professor [chairman of the Pudong Development Corporation]

I turned to the driver and said, with a sigh, "I do whatever comes next."

Introduction

I start with Tennessee Williams (1911–1983), who moved to New Orleans in 1939, and saw the community as a fascinating backdrop for plays that depict the death of the old South and the emergence of a troubled people and place. There were litanies of famous and infamous people born and raised in New Orleans from musicians to artists. As the crucible of so much talent the city has sadly not been able to hold or build fortunes on that talent. Huey Long was at constant war with the *Times-Picayune*. In November 1933, he warned the daily newspapers in a speech in Marksville, "Take those lying *Times-Picayune*, *Shreveport Times*, and *Alexandria Town Talk*. We are going to sock a tax on those damned rascals"; see Richard White, *Kingfish: The Reign of Huey P. Long* (Random House, 2006). The tragic history and results of the hurricanes that have struck the New Orleans area are documented in "Hurricanes in Louisiana History," http://www.thecajuns.com/lahurricanes.htm. The decline of the New Orleans economy has been repeatedly and well documented. The poor structural characters of the levees protecting New Orleans have been explored in numerous books and reports. The most authoritative work here is Anuradha Mathur and Dilip da Cunha, "Negotiating a Fluid Terrain," in Eugenie L. Birch and Susan M. Wachter, eds., *Rebuilding Urban Places After Disaster: Lessons from Hurricane Katrina* (University of Pennsylvania, Press, 2006), 34–45.

Oliver Houck, a Tulane University student, is cited from Joel K. Bourne, Jr., "New Orleans: A Perilous Future," *National Geographic* 212, 2 (August 2007): 43, a very compelling examination of the fragile state of the levee system which the *National Geographic* editor says "was a man made disaster that began with the founding of New Orleans in 1718." One of the best accounts of the drama and trauma of the flood period is contained in Dave Eggers, *Zeitoun* (Vintage, 2010), where the tale of confusion and disarray of public institutions in and outside the city is laid bare.

This book is intended to be a sequel to the great work by Jeffrey Pressman and Aaron Wildavsky, *Implementation: How Great Expectations in Washington Are Dashed in Oakland or Why It's Amazing That Federal Programs Work at All* (University of California Press, 1973 and updated). It tells a familiar story of differing expectations dashing hope and creating confusion.

The book picks up from where Robert Olshansky and Laurie Johnson leave off in *Clear as Mud: Planning for the Rebuilding of New Orleans* (American Planning Association, 2010). Nicole Gelinas pulls together post-Katrina in "Will New Orleans Recover? Weak and Struggling Before Katrina, the Good-Time City Now Teeters on the Brink," *City Journal*, August 31, 2005.

Chapter 1: An Alarming View from Down Under

Lionel Wilson was the first African American mayor of Oakland, California, and a legend in his own time for his work with the poor and his love and contributions to sports. His life story is best viewed in the University of California oral history *Attorney, Judge, and Oakland Mayor: Oral History Transcript/ Lionel Wilson; with an Introduction by Professor Edward J. Blakely; Interviews conducted by Gabrielle Morris in 1985, 1990* (Regional Oral History Office, Bancroft Library, University of California, Berkeley, 1992). Information on the Oakland Earthquake can be found in Jane Gross, "Oakland's Dowdy Image Is Shattered," Special to the *New York Times*, November 7, 1989; my role with Elihu Harris is in Gross, "Oakland Struggles to Restore Hill and Faith," *New York Times*, October 26, 1991.

Chapter 2: Getting to New Orleans

This chapter, like a Russian novel, introduces most of the players in the narrative. They all have information on the web that provides context as to what they do and who they are. This note provides the reader with a guide to the parts they played in my narrative.

The American Planning Association (APA) is the peak body for professionals who practice land use and urban design and related government regulated planning and zoning in the United States. I have been a member for four decades, and it is my professional home organization. Its primary office, unlike those of many professional organizations, is in Chicago, not Washington. The location is a bit symbolic of the origins of the profession in the American heartland. APA puts out a scholarly journal and newsletter and I have contributed to both as well as using its resources for much of my daily work. Paul Farmer, executive director, is highly regarded and very hard working. He personally led the efforts to get the APA engaged in New Orleans after Katrina.

The Federal Emergency Management Agency (FEMA), as everyone in America knows, is the organization responsible for meeting community needs when a disaster strikes. It was reorganized under President Bush and merged with Homeland Security. While this is a logical fit, in an emergency this structure needlessly complicates decision making and delivery of services to needy communities.

Marvin Olasky, *The Politics of Disaster: Katrina, Big Government and a New Strategy for Future Crises* (W Publishing, 2006) is a useful description of the political paralysis of Katrina. Olasky provides good evidence that the tales of rape and mayhem in the Superdome and the city were greatly exaggerated by the press. One might not agree with Olasky's politics, but his reporting is well done. Jed Horne, *Breach of Faith: Hurricane Katrina and New Orleans* (Random House, 2008) (by the former editor of the *Times-Picayune*) is a useful source. There are a myriad other eye-catching works on the storm and its aftermath, including Spike Lee's documentary *When the Levees Broke: A Requiem in Four Acts*.

Chapter 3: A Harbinger of Problems to Come

The history of the New Orleans Redevelopment Authority (NORA) is on its website. As to its role when I was there, the only source that makes reference to it is Robert B. Olshanky and Laurie Johnson, *Clear as Mud: Planning for the Rebuilding of New Orleans* (APA, 2010). NORA's primary role to process vacant properties. But New Orleans bureaucracy and Louisiana law made this an almost impossible task since each vacant abandoned property had to be purchased at a "fair market" value and funds out of a trust.

The Unified New Orleans Plan (UNOP) and the Lambert planning effort are documented very extensively by Olshansky and Johnson. I used much of their data to develop the final target area plans, and used the population information provided by Greg Rigamer, who reinforced the information provided by the UNOP team. Some flap erupted in Sydney when I mentioned these numbers that showed actual resident population below the official census and pointed out that higher numbers are always best in the U.S. to protect revenue sharing. Rigamer and later the local community census organization used mail drops to augment their totals, which remained low until well into 2009. The following NPR report provides a very good picture of what was and what is likely to come: http://marketplace.publicradio.org/display/web/2010/08/30/pm-building-new-orleans-longterm-future-still-a-struggle/. One of the best places to look at the population past, present, and future is Greg Rigamer, GCR population estimates at www.gcrconsulting.com.

Chapter 4: "Fix It!"

The Battle of New Orleans was fought during the War of 1812 against the British Army to control New Orleans to secure the Louisiana Purchase of 1804. This battle is often regarded as the greatest American land victory of the war. Recovery from Katrina would represent a very similar effort. The scale of the disaster is well documented in numerous works. My own background as a recovery expert can be viewed on the University of California at Riverside website for the Blakely Center for Sustainable Suburban Development and elsewhere. A great deal has been recorded about the Katrina flood tragedy. Among the best work is Jed Horne's *Breach of Faith*.

Chapter 5: Imagining a Future Out of Mud: A Recovery Plan

The two best works on pre- and immediately post-Katrina politics and planning challenges are Chapters 6–12 in Birch and Wachter, *Rebuilding Urban Places* and Olshanky and Johnson, *Clear as Mud*.

Chapter 6: Inside the Mayor's "Cocoon"

Leaders and leadership are changing. I tried to use "soft power," the style advocated by Joseph Nye of the Harvard JFK School of Government in the *The Powers to Lead* (Oxford University Press, 2008). Leadership through persuasion and influence is the path favored by leaders who use soft power to manage. I am a long-standing advocate of soft power, but it is just one way to manage. Success is obtained with smart power by combining hard and soft power skills in varying proportions, depending on the situation. Leadership with soft power transforms group members through the use of attraction, inspiration, persuasion, and charisma. Leaders who are better at using smart power have contextual intelligence. They know when to use soft or hard power to inspire their followers since they are aware of the distribution of power in their organization, its cultural values, and changes in their followers' needs.

Hard power is more appropriate when there is a need to appeal to tangible interests, whereas soft power is effective when a leader can appeal to higher order values and noble purposes.

The most important and influential ideas for this chapter came from Doris Kearn Goodwin, *A Team of Rivals: The Political Genius of Abraham Lincoln* (Simon and Schuster, 2005)

Chapter 7: Putting My Team on the Field: Recovery Administration

Pressman and Wildavsky's *Implementations* is the book I referred to most as I crafted an organization to meet the local needs and to battle with the Washington bureaucracy.

Chapter 8: Politics and Money

HUD's role in first taking over and later deciding to raze public housing in New Orleans has been chronicled in many places. One good article is Lewis Wallace, "First Came Katrina, Then Came HUD: Activists Battle to Save New Orleans Public Housing," *These Times*, January 16, 2008, http://www.inthese-times.com/article/3504/first_came_katrina_then_came_hud/. The Louisiana Recovery Authority, my role and presentations to it for funds, and the other funding sources I sought are documented in Olshanky and Johnson, *Clear as Mud*. Note should be taken of the description of the relationship between Powell and Voelker: "so in effect, Voelker—in pressing for a unified, citywide plan—was actually representing Powell," 266. In essence, from the White House to New Orleans there was a game plan to use the funds (nonprofit) to allocate them, thus bypassing the elected leadership of the city.

I have documented all communications regarding the attempt to move funds to nonprofit including emails, notes, and telephone logs.

Chapter 9: Reviving a Drowning Economy

The New Orleans economy and its opportunities and deficits are the subject of very little scholarly or policy research. What research there is tends to focus on tourism or the decline of the regional economy. This is surprising, given the number of universities in the city with strong regional economics departments. For my work I was forced to use reports from the regional economic organization Greater New Orleans Inc. Data on employment from 1960–2000 are drawn from the U.S. Census.

Susan L. Cutter and Christopher T. Emrich, "Moral Hazard, Social Catastrophe: The Changing Face of Vulnerability Along the Hurricane Coasts,"

ANNALS of the American Academy of Political and Social Science 604 (2006): 102. Isabel V. Sawhill, vice president and director of economic studies at the Brookings Institution, provides a sobering reflection on the state of and potential for the New Orleans economy, http://dir.salon.com/story/news/feature/2005/09/30/rebuild_reaction/index2.html. *Newsweek*, January 21, 2011, ranked New Orleans as one of America's Dying Cities, http://www.newsweek.com/2011/01/21/americas-dying-cities.html

The MOU with the VA is included as the Appendix .

Chapter 10: In Search of Civic Leadership

This chapter draws heavily on the work in Lawrence Vale and Thomas J. Campanella, *The Resilient City: How Modern Cities Recover from Disaster* (Oxford University Press, 2005). My colleague Robert Putnam's powerful work on civic engagement that transforms communities, *Bowling Alone: The Collapse and Revival of American Social Capital* (Simon & Schuster, 2000) is particularly applicable to New Orleans, and his *Democracies in Flux: The Evolution of Social Capital* (Oxford University Press, 2002) makes the point for all communities, since every city faces new natural and potential man-made catastrophe.

SPUR, the San Francisco Planning and Urban Research Association, is one of many suggested models of civic leadership organizations that bind communities together to seek common goals. SPUR's history and current program can be found on its website www.spur.org/.

Chapter 11: More Than Bricks and Sticks: Reviving Neighborhoods

Information on all the organizations cited in this chapter can be found on the Web. The Brookings New Orleans Index is an excellent resource on the internal rebuilding of the city: New Orleans, Natural Disasters, Cities, Community Development, http://www.brookings.edu/topics/new-orleans.aspx. See Thomas J. Campanella, "Urban Resilience and the Recovery of New Orleans," *Journal of the American Planning Association* 72, 2 (Spring 2006): 142. See Olshanky and Johnson, 284 n 62, for discussion of population return. Even as late as February 2011, Michele Krupa of the *Times-Picayune* was using this illogical argument to suggest I had underestimated the city's return of residents when I simply used the arithmetic Olshanky laid out.

Chapter 12: The Race Cards of Recovery

Data on black-white differences are taken from a variety of sources, including U.S. Census, *Nation's Richest and Poorest Cities*, 2009. William Frey and

Dowell Myers, among the nation's leading demographers, place New Orleans among the most social/racially segregated cities in the nation; see Social Data Analysis Network (SSDAN); Center on Budget and Policy Priorities September 19, 2005; Earl Hutchinson, "The Real Reasons New Orleans Is So Poor" for racism and the continuing local and state policies, http://www.alternet.org/katrina/25277/. Phyllis Landrieu, former chair of the New Orleans school board, adds the dismal statistics on black youth outcomes.

Rep. Jefferson's troubles with an indictment for corruption and bribery are well documented in many sources, particularly in the *Times-Picayune* throughout 2008 and 2009. See Richard Morin, "Study Participants Favor Whites over Blacks for Katrina Relief Aid," *Washington Post*, Saturday, June 10, 2006, A-5; John Berry, *Rising Tide: The Great Mississippi Flood of 1927 and How It Changed America* (Simon and Schuster, 1997); William Goldsmith and Edward Blakely, *Separate Societies: Poverty and Inequality in U.S. Cities* (Temple University Press, 2010), 110; Eijah Anderson, "Inadequate Responses, Limited Expectations," in Birch and Wachter, 199; Olshansky and Johnson, 219; Berry, 279.

Chapter 13: A Medium Off Message

"The medium is the message" is a phrase coined by Marshall McLuhan meaning that the form of a medium embeds itself in the message, creating a symbiotic relationship. The phrase was introduced in his most widely known book, *Understanding Media: The Extension of Man* (originally published in 1964 by Mentor, reissued by MIT Press, 1994, with an introduction by Lewis Lapham). McLuhan proposes that a medium itself, not the content it carries, should be the focus of study, that a medium affects the society in which it plays a role not only by the content delivered but also by the characteristics of the medium itself (Wikipedia, 2010).

Chapter 14: Levees and FEMA: The Real Hazards for New Orleans

This chapter draws on two sources: Vale and Campanella, *Resilient Cities*, and the National Academy of Sciences report by Robert W. Kates, C. E. Colten, Shirley B. Laska, and S. P. Leatherman, *Reconstruction of New Orleans After Hurricane Katrina: A Research Perspective*, an Internet resource, doi:10.1073/pnas.0605726103, September 26, 2006, on New Orleans and other disasters (information current as of September 2006), and data I found at the Disaster Prevention Research Institute, Kyoto University, Japan.

This chapter also draws on the work of Ivor van Heerden, *The Storm: What*

Went Wrong and Why During Hurricane Katrina: The Inside Story from One Louisiana Scientist (Viking, 2006). Van Heerden has clung to the fact that the levees were breached because of incompetent construction, and that the Corps program to rectify this failure is equally wrongheaded and doomed to fail. I draw heavily on the epic battle over the use of levees as the preferred technique for corralling the Mississippi from Berry's *Rising Tide* and several scientists' work that appears in Birch and Wachter, *Rebuilding Urban Places*.

To make sure my conclusions made scientific sense, I ran them by Doug Meffert, Tulane University Xavier Center for Bioenvironmental Research, who lives and works on the issues discussed, and Tim McDaniels, University of British Columbia School of Community and Regional Planning, who studies risk management for disasters and knows the issues of the Mississippi. In addition my colleagues in Japan at the Disaster Prevention Institute have data and GIS resources as sophisticated as the Corps of Engineers. They endorsed my proposals conceptually but some had a hard time with the politics of implementation, given the entrenched interests that got van Heerden fired from a tenured post at Louisiana State University.

Chapter 15: Assessing the Recovery

Harvard has a long tradition of inviting active professionals to give talks and using these talks as the basis (with other materials) for the Harvard Case Studies. My work was featured in at least one case study and I have been interviewed for others. My talk at Harvard JFK was given on May 9, 2009; the data were featured by the Office of Recovery and Development Administration in 2009.

Chapter 16: In the "Big Easy," Nothing Comes Easy, Not Even Leaving

The majority of the material for this chapter can be found on the United States Studies Centre website at the University of Sydney. My own background with the U.S. Foreign Service included a stint as senior reserve foreign service officer in 1967–70 and short-term assignments in 1978–2003 on diplomatic missions with USAID, State Department, and other international agencies.

Memorandum of Understanding

MEMORANDUM OF UNDERSTANDING

The United States Department of Veterans Affairs

And

The City of New Orleans, Louisiana

Regarding A

Potential VA Enhanced-Use Lease of the

Southeast Louisiana Veterans Healthcare System

VA Medical Center In New Orleans, Louisiana

To the City of New Orleans

And

A Potential Acquisition and Transfer of Certain

New Orleans Land by the City of New Orleans to VA

For the Construction and Operation

Of A New VA Medical Center

MEMORANDUM OF UNDERSTANDING

PREAMBLE

This Memorandum of Understanding (**"MOU"**) dated _____, _____ 200___, is by and between the Secretary of Veterans Affairs, on behalf of the United States Department of Veterans Affairs (the **"Department"** or **"VA"**) and the City of New Orleans, Louisiana (the **"City"**), and such entities may collectively be referred to herein as the **"Parties."**

RECITALS

A. **WHEREAS,** the Department currently has a VA hospital known as "The Southeast Louisiana Veterans Healthcare System VA Medical Center" (the **"VAMC"**) located in New Orleans Louisiana;

B.   **WHEREAS,** the VAMC and VA's underlying mission and hospital operations there were significantly affected by the storm surge of Hurricane Katrina (**"Hurricane"**) that impacted the City in August 2005;

C.   **WHEREAS,** due to such Hurricane affects, VA has identified the need for and now is seeking to legally obtain a new land site in the City on which to build and then operate a new, world-class VA hospital and related facilities (**"New VAMC"**), and is interested in the possibility of outleasing the VAMC to a public or private entity for a term of up to 75 years pursuant and subject to its Enhanced-Use (**"EU"**) Lease statute (i.e., 38 U.S.C. §§ 8161-8169) appearing at **"Attachment A"**;

D.   **WHEREAS,** the City has approached VA by a written, letter offer dated August 16, 2007 (the **"City Letter"** appearing at **Attachment "B"**), which details certain provisions whereby the City would obtain and make legally available to VA a targeted developable and usable area of land in the City that consists of approximately 34 acres (the **"34-Acre Site"**), is comprised of an area bounded by Rochblave (north), Galvez (south), Tulane (west), and Canal (east), and whereon VA could construct and operate its New VAMC;

E.   **WHEREAS,** the City has indicated to VA an interest in obtaining a leasehold interest in or ownership of the VAMC property if it is made available by VA via its EU leasing authority or some other legal means;

F.   **WHEREAS,** a New VAMC would be consistent with the pertinent part of Department's mission of providing veterans located in the City and southeastern Louisiana with the high quality healthcare services they deserve and expect, and serve as a vital component for the long-term recovery of medical care and services available in the City;

G.   **WHEREAS,** the "Division of Administration of the State of Louisiana" (per **Attachment "C"**); the "New Orleans City Planning Commission" (per **Attachment "D"**); the "Sewer and Water Board of New Orleans" (per **Attachment "E"**); and "Entergy New Orleans, Inc. (i.e., a private electric company in part serving customers in New Orleans) (per **Attachment "F"**), have all expressed positive support and interest in VA being able to successfully build and operate a New VAMC; and

H.   **WHEREAS,** the Parties now agree per Paragraph "q" of the City Letter, to memorialize in this MOU their revised present understanding of the key terms and conditions regarding the City's offer to obtain and make the 34-Acre Site legally available to VA for constructing and operating its New VAMC, and VA's potential future EU Lease of the VAMC to the City.

NOW THEREFORE, consistent with the foregoing Recitals, VA and the City hereby agree to the following Stipulations:

STIPULATIONS
---

1.   VA shall have a unilateral right to issue a written notice to the City (**"VA Land Acquisition Notice"**), instructing the City (with assistance from the Division of Administration of the State of Louisiana, hereafter referred to as the "Division") to initiate the acquisition of and to acquire fee simple title to the 34-Acre Site per Attachment D, all at no cost or expense to VA. The City shall have thirty (30) days following issuance of the VA Land Acquisition Notice to notify the Division in writing (and provide a courtesy copy to VA) that the City and the Division must then initiate and complete the land acquisition process. If the City fails to so notify the Division (and provide a courtesy copy to VA) within such thirty (30) days, such failure shall constitute a material breach under this MOU, and the City shall immediately owe and pay VA MOU Damages as defined in Stipulation #25 below.

2.   The Parties agree that the City intends to use funds provided by the State of Louisiana to acquire the 34-Acre Site, and should those funds not be available, the City shall complete the acquisition using its own funds and shall not in any manner either delay the acquisition or in any manner alter the commitment contained herein.

3.   The City shall secure fee simple title to the 34-Acre Site at no cost or expense to VA and notify VA of the same in writing within 365 days from the date that VA issues the VA Land Acquisition Notice to the City (the **"365-Day Period"**). If the City fails to do so within the 365-Day Period, such failure shall constitute a material breach under this MOU, and the City shall immediately owe and pay VA MOU Damages as defined in Stipulation #25 below.

4.   In addition to the City's requirements set forth in Stipulation #3 above, the City shall accomplish (or cause the accomplishment of) the following tasks at no cost or expense to VA within the 365-Day Period:

a.   A Phase I Environmental Site Assessment (ESA) and, if the Phase I ESA identifies the likely release or presence of any Hazardous Substances, a Phase II ESA and, if the Phase II ESA identifies the need for remediation or abatement,a full remediation of any Hazardous Substances discovered on the 34-Acre Site. "Hazardous Substance," and "release" shall have the same meanings and definitions set forth in the Federal Resource Conservation and Recovery Act of 1976, 42 U.S.C. §§ 6901, *et seq.*, the Federal Comprehensive Environmental Response, Compensation and Liability Act of 1980, 42 U.S.C. Sections 9601, *et seq.*, and all amendments thereto including, without limitation, the Superfund Amendments and Reauthorization Act of 1986, the Federal Clean Water Act, 33 U.S.C. Sections 445, *et seq.*, the Emergency Planning and Community Right to know Act, 42 U.S.C. Section 11001, et seq., the Hazardous Materials Transportation Act, 49 U.S.C. Sections 1801, *et seq.*, the Toxic Substances Control Act, 15 U.S.C. Sections 2601, et seq., and any state laws of similar applicability to which the New VAMC site is subject, all as amended from time to time, and in accordance with any regulations now promulgated under any of the foregoing, or under any other existing Federal, State or local law, statute, ordinance, code, rule, regulation, order, or decree regulating, relating to, or imposing liability or standards of conduct concerning any hazardous, toxic or dangerous waste, substance or material, including, without limitation, asbestos, polychlorinate biphenyls, medical waste, petroleum, or source, special nuclear or by-product materials as defined by the Atomic Energy Act of 1954,42 U.S.C. Sections 3011, *et seq.*, as amended, as now in effect.

b.   All existing improvements and pavement must be removed from the 34-Acre Site, including any subsurface structures or tanks, and shall deliver the 34-Acre Site to VA in a construction-ready state. Construction-ready state, for the purposes of this MOU, shall be defined as causing VA to undertake no other efforts prior to commencing its construction than those it would undertake on a parcel of land that had never previously been developed

c.   All major water and sewer lines traversing within the boundaries of the 34-Acre Site must be removed and/or relocated off the 34-Acre Site, so as to permit VA's unencumbered use of the 34-Acre Site.

d.   The construction of any necessary facilities and infrastructure off-site from and on-site of the boundaries of the 34-Acre Site, which are necessary to deliver adequate and reliable underground electrical power and natural gas to the 34-Acre Site.

e.   The Parties acknowledge that there exists an abandoned Dixie Brewery (**"Dixie Brewery"**) within the boundaries of the 34-Acre Site, which has previously been awarded historic designation. That historic designation may prohibit VA's economic use of the land under the Dixie Brewery. So, prior to the expiration of the 365-Day Period, VA shall advise the City in writing of VA's plans regarding the future of the Dixie Brewery. Specifically, if VA advises the City that the inclusion of the Dixie Brewery facility on the 34-Acre Site is inconsistent with VA's development plans, the Dixie Brewery will be removed and thereafter excluded from the boundaries of the 34-Acre Site at no cost or penalty to VA. Further, if VA expressly requests the City, the City will take all necessary steps to expeditiously identify, obtain, and provide VA (within the One-Year Post VA Plan Delivery Day Period as defined in Stipulation #8 below, or such other time as the Parties agree) with fee simple title to an approximately equal "replacement acreage" of land (to become part of the 34-Acre Site) for the New VAMC.

5.   If the City fails to accomplish (or cause the accomplishment

of) any of the tasks identified in Stipulations #3 and/or #4 above within the 365-Day Period, such failure shall constitute a material breach under this MOU, and the City shall immediately owe and pay VA MOU Damages as defined in Stipulation #25 below.

6.   Within twenty (20) days of accomplishing (or causing the accomplishment) of each task identified in Stipulations #3 and #4 above, the City shall advise and confirm the same to VA in writing. Additionally, within twenty (20) days of accomplishing (or causing the accomplishment) of all the tasks identified in Stipulations #3 and #4 above, the City shall advise and confirm the same to VA in writing (the **"City's All Tasks Completed Notice for MOU Stipulations #3 and #4"**).

7.   Following the City's issuance of the City's All Tasks Completed Notice for MOU Stipulations #3 and #4, VA shall when they become available provide the City with a copy of its final architectural and engineering plans (the **"A&E Plans"**) for the New VAMC. The day VA that provides the A&E Plans to the City shall hereinafter be referred to as the **"VA Plan Delivery Day."** Within 1-year (i.e., 365 days) following the VA Plan Delivery Day (the **"One-Year Post VA Plan Delivery Day Period"**), the City shall accomplish (or cause the accomplishment of) the following tasks at no cost or expense to VA (unless and to the extent expressly set forth below), all in a manner that is in coordination with the A&E Plans and VA's targeted completion of and opening date for the New VAMC:

> a.   Construction of any necessary facilities and infrastructure off-site from and on-site within the boundaries of the 34-Acre Site, which are necessary to deliver adequate and reliable domestic water, sanitary sewer, and storm water drainage infrastructure to the 34-Acre Site, and repair or replacement of any portions of existing infrastructure located remote from the 34-Acre Site that VA's professional consultants and/or engineers determine jeopardize the potential reliability of the supply of domestic water or the removal of sanitary sewer or storm water. The City will cause all of the work in this Clause "c" to be done by the New Orleans Sewerage and Water Board.

b.   All streets feeding the 34-Acre Site as well as those streets adjacent thereto must be improved to the degree reasonably necessary to accommodate traffic whose destination is the 34-Acre Site as well as the traffic passing through the area. The term reasonably necessary improvements used in this context will be defined as those improvements deemed appropriate by an accredited, independent traffic engineer mutually-selected by VA and the City on a 50/50 fee split basis. The report shall recognize the traffic impact of the proposed development of an LSU medical teaching facility on the land to the south of the 34-Acre Site, and any other traffic impacts deemed relevant by the engineer.

c.   Relocate all businesses and residences from the 34-Acre Site as may be required under the Uniform Relocation Assistance and Real Property Acquisition Policies Act of 1970, 42 U.S.C. § 4620, and/or applicable State and/or local law.

8.   The Parties acknowledge that there exists along Rochblave Street within the boundaries of the 34-Acre Site, a sewer pumping facility operated by the Sewerage and Water Board (**"Sewer Pumping Facility"**). Concurrently with VA providing the A&E Plans to the City on the VA Plan Delivery Date, VA shall advise the City of VA's plans regarding the future of the Sewer Pumping Facility. Specifically, if VA advises the City on the VA Plan Delivery Day that VA requires that the Sewer Pumping Facility be removed because VA has an alternative use for the land upon which the Sewer Pumping Facility rests, the City shall upon receiving such notice from VA and within the **One-Year Post VA Plan Delivery Day Period**, cause the facility to be relocated at no cost or expense to VA.

9.   If the City fails to accomplish (or cause the accomplishment of) any of the tasks identified in Stipulations #7 and #8 within the One-Year Post VA Plan Delivery Day Period, such failure shall constitute a material breach under this MOU, and the City shall immediately owe and pay VA MOU Damages as defined in Stipulation #25 below.

10.   Within twenty (20) days of accomplishing (or causing the accomplishment) of each task identified in Stipulations #7 and #8 as is or

may be required by each of those Stipulations, the City shall advise and confirm the same to VA in writing. Additionally, within twenty (20) days of accomplishing (or causing the accomplishment) of <u>all</u> the tasks identified in Stipulations #3 and #4 above, the City shall advise and confirm the same to VA in writing (the **"City's All Tasks Completed Notice for MOU Stipulations #7 and #8"**).

11.   Within ten (10) days after the City has completed all of its obligations or requirements as set forth in Stipulations #1, #2, #3, #4, #6, #7, and #8 above, it shall issue a written letter granting VA the option of selecting one of the following three options for occupying and using the 34-Acre Site (the **"City's Land Use Option Letter"**): (a) Option 1—VA receiving a fee simple title transfer of the land from the City with no conditions or restrictions; (b) Option 2—VA receiving a fee simple title transfer of the land from the City at no cost as part of the lease consideration to be provided by the City to VA under an EU lease of the VAMC to the City (if the City can in fact be and is awarded the EU Lease by VA per the EU Lease statute and pertinent VA policy); or (c) Option 3—VA leasing the 34-Acre Site for a term to be determined by VA in accordance with its leasing authorities, per a nominal rent (i.e., $1/year). VA shall advise of its desired option in writing to the City within 90 days (or within such other time period that the Parties may otherwise agree to in writing), and such notice shall be referred to herein as the **"VA Reply To the City's Land Use Option Letter."**

12.   As a condition of this MOU and the City issuing VA the City Land Use Option Letter, and regardless of which of the three options in Stipulation #11 that VA ultimately selects, the City hereby recognizes that that VA typically develops its medical centers on property titled in the United States that is under VA's jurisdiction and control, which are not subject to or encumbered by State and local zoning, building and other codes, and permitting requirements. In that regard, the City hereby agrees that as a condition of any option selected by VA (and as may also be consistent with the Louisiana Revised Statute 52:1 at **Attachment "G"**), the City will expressly and unconditionally grant VA an exemption from all New Orleans municipal zoning, building and other codes, and permitting requirements. Such exemption(s) shall allow the United States and VA to develop the Site in any manner it deems desirable, except that the Parties recognize that VA is obligated to comply with Federal laws, codes, ordi-

nances, and regulations, including but not limited to, the National Building Codes (40 U.S.C. § 3312).

13.   If VA indicates in its VA Reply To the City's Land Use Option Letter issued to the City (per Stipulation #11 above), that VA has selected Option 2, VA and the City will engage in good faith negotiations commencing ninety (90) days after issuance of such letter, in an effort to agree upon the key deal points for a VA EU lease of the VAMC to the City. In that regard, the Parties already have agreed as follows:

a.   Under the EU lease, VA shall deliver possession of the VAMC property to the City on an 'as is, where is' basis.

b.   The EU lease shall provide for transfer of the VAMC property to the City in at least two phases, such that VA shall have the right to retain occupancy and usage of certain portions of the VAMC for and until such time that corresponding facilities at the New VAMC are ready for VA's use and occupancy.

14.   The Parties acknowledge and agree that in order for an EU lease of the VAMC to be completed by VA to the City, the EU lease process requires that certain statutory requirements ("**EU Lease Statutory Requirements**") be completed by VA (with assistance from the City as and to the extent VA and the City agree), including the need for a VA public hearing and its issuance of congressional notifications that have stipulated minimum waiting periods after such notices are issued.

15.   Within twenty (20) days of VA completing the EU Lease Statutory Requirements, it shall advise the City in writing.

16.   The Parties agree that in the event VA selects an option other than Option 2 described in Stipulation #11 above, or VA selects such Option 2 and thereafter VA and the City are unable to consummate an EU lease of the VAMC campus from VA to the City, then VA shall have the option and right to occupy and use the 34-Acre Site per either Option 1 or Option 3 as discussed in Stipulation #11 above. VA shall notify the City of this Option selection within ten (10) days of the date that the Parties' EU lease negotia-

tions have conclusively ceased (i.e., such date as agreed to by the Parties in writing).

17.   The Parties hereby agree to cooperate in good faith for all purposes of this MOU, and regularly and in advance to the extent practicable and reasonable when discussing this MOU verbally or in writing with third parties. Further, in that regard, each party shall provide the other party for reasonable review and comment, advance copies of any draft written correspondence addressed to third parties or to be released into the public domain, which discusses or regards this MOU.

18.   **Dispute Resolution Process:**

a.   VA and the City acknowledge and agree that disputes under this MOU shall be resolved under the Contract Disputes Act of 1978 (41 U.S.C. Sec. 601-613) (the "Disputes Act"), and that both VA and the City will utilize "Alternative Dispute Resolution" procedures on all matters appealed by either of them to the Civilian Board of Contract Appeals, and any successor authority thereto), to the extent permitted under the Disputes Act, unless the parties then should otherwise agree.

b.   In the event that the Disputes Act is not available or permissible under applicable law to resolve a dispute under this Lease, VA and the City shall, to the extent permitted by applicable law and regulation, resolve the dispute by arbitration. In that regard, the arbitration shall take place in Washington, D.C. unless the Department and Lessee otherwise agree in writing.

c.   Each party shall be responsible for and shall bear their own costs and expenses (including attorney's fees and costs) incurred in the course of pursuing and resolving disputes pursuant to this Stipulation #18. Furthermore, notwithstanding anything in this MOU to the contrary, VA and the City hereby agree that the scope of any and all monetary disputes, claims, and penalties payable by either party against the other under this MOU shall be limited to a maximum, capped amount of five million dollars ($5,000,000.00).

19.   The term (**"Term"**) of this MOU shall commence beginning on the date that the parties affix their signatures below (provided that, if it is signed on different days, the term shall commence as of the date of the second party's signature), which date shall be the **"MOU Commencement Date"** of this MOU, and then automatically expire (with no further action of VA or the City being necessary) at 12:00 midnight EST on Friday, June 1, 2013 (the **"MOU Termination Date"**), provided that if, on June 1, 2013, the Parties mutually determine that their efforts as contemplated herein are progressing such that an extension to this MOU is warranted, then they shall proceed to formally extend the MOU Termination Date.

20.   In addition to any other provisions herein granting VA a right to expressly terminate this MOU upon certain acts or omissions of the City, the Parties agree that if one party to this MOU (the **"Affected Party"**) in its good faith determines that the other party is failing to adequately and timely pursue and/or achieve its respective obligations herein, or has materially breached the MOU, the Affected Party may, subject to Stipulation #18 above, terminate this MOU upon sixty (60) days written notice to the other Party. At the discretion of the Parties, the Secretary of VA and the Mayor of the City may opt during such 60-day notice period and any additional period that may be provided pursuant to the dispute process in Stipulation #18 above, endeavor to resolve any outstanding dispute.

21.   The Parties agree that for purposes of their moving forward as contemplated herein, the Parties will follow the sequence of events and terms and conditions of this Agreement, rather than the body of the City Letter referenced in Recital D above.

22.   The City agrees during the Term of this MOU to use its best efforts and take those actions that are necessary to maintain (along with VA) the positive support and interest that the entities and organizations cited in the above Recital G have expressed for VA hopefully in the near future being able to build and operate a New VAMC, and to promote and sustain positive community relations for purposes of the steps, goals, and objectives contemplated herein.

23.   For purposes of this MOU, "Force Majeure" means any of the following that directly cause either of the Parties' obligations hereunder not to be performed in a timely manner: (a) an earthquake, hurricane, tornado, flood, or other similar act of God; (b) fire; (c) strikes or similar labor disputes provided such strike or similar dispute is beyond the control of the affected party and provided that affected party takes all steps reasonably possible to remediate such strike or similar dispute; (d) acts of the public enemy; (v) inability to obtain labor or materials or clear access to the VAMC property and/or the New VAMC site, as applicable, by reason of acts or omissions of any governmental body not caused by the affected party's actions or omissions; (e) rebellions, riots, insurrections or civil unrest; (f) unusually severe weather conditions that actually cause similar construction or development activities in the area of the VAMC property and/or the New VAMC site to be suspended; (g) discovery, remediation, and abatement of any unknown environmental hazard or unknown hazardous substance (i.e., a hazardous substance, covered by any environmental law or regulation, whose existence on the Property is unknown to Department or the City despite appropriate environmental studies as required by this MOU and/or applicable Federal, State, or local law, codes, ordinances, and regulations and which is affecting the VAMC property (with VA as the affected party) and/or the New VAMC site (with the City as the affected party); (h) discovery of any ancient, historical, archeological, architectural, or cultural artifacts, relics, or remains on the VAMC property (with VA as the affected party) and/or the New VAMC site (with the City as the affected party); and (i) any act or omission of a governmental body other than VA and the City not caused by either VA's or the City's actions or omissions.

24.   Appropriations. Any obligation of VA to pay any money pursuant to or under this MOU is subject to appropriation by the Congress of the United States of America of the necessary funds. Without limiting the foregoing, consistent with the Anti-Deficiency Act (31 U.S.C. §§ 1341 and 1501), the rules adopted thereunder, and any successors thereto, the indemnification obligations of VA shall not exceed appropriations available to VA which can be lawfully expended for such purposes at the time of the claim; and nothing in this MOU may be construed as implying that Congress will at a later date appropriate funds to meet any deficiencies. Any obligation of the City to pay any money pursuant to or under this MOU is subject to

the applicable appropriation laws, codes, ordinances, and regulations of the State of Louisiana and the City of New Orleans.

25.   The Parties recognize that the veterans to be served at the contemplated New VAMC site may receive healthcare and services of a level that is not of the high quality that VA intends to deliver, if the City fails to timely meet its obligations herein. Accordingly, in such an instance and subject to Stipulation #18 above, in such event where there is a material breach by the City in its obligations that in VA's view rises to the level that veteran care will be adversely and significantly affected by the City's lapse(s) under this MOU, the City will immediately owe, and pay (i.e., in no event later than fifteen (15) days after the corresponding City breach under this MOU occurs) VA monetary (i.e., liquidated, non-penalty damages) ("MOU Damages") to the extent that applicable Federal, State, and local law allows. Such damages shall be based upon $1,000/day for the first week, $2,000/day for the second week, $3,000/day for the third week, $4,000/day for the fourth week, $5,000/day for the fifth week, $6,000/day for the sixth week, $7,000/day for the seventh week, $8,000/day for the eighth week, $9,000/day for the ninth week, and $10,000/day for each day thereafter that the City is late performing any of its obligations in this MOU. The Parties agree that the preceding dollar amounts best approximate the monetary damages that will fall upon VA as a result of the City's delays under this MOU, and more precise approximations are presently unascertainable. The Parties further agree that VA's rights to receive MOU Damages and the City's obligation to pay them in accordance with and subject to this Stipulation #25 shall survive the termination or expiration of this MOU. Lastly, the Parties agree that in addition to the rights afforded and favoring VA in the preceding sentence, if and when the City breaches this MOU, at VA's sole and absolute discretion, it shall have the right to immediately terminate this MOU and all of VA's obligations herein, via a written notice to the City.

26.   The Parties hereby represent that each in its individual capacity has duly approved, executed, and delivered this MOU by all legally requisite action.

27.   No agreement shall be effective to amend, change, modify, waive, release, discharge, or terminate this MOU, in whole or in part, unless such agreement is in writing, refers expressly to the MOU, and is

duly signed by VA and the City. Furthermore, no rights hereunder may be waived except in writing by the waiving party to the other party of this MOU.

     IN WITNESS WHEREOF, the parties hereto have hereunto subscribed their names as of the date first above written.

The United States Department of Veterans Affairs

By:_____   Date: _____

Name:_____

Title:_____

The City of New Orleans, Louisiana

Representative #1

By:_____   Date: _____

Name:_____

Title:_____

DATE DUE

SEP 1 0 2012	